A Square Peg

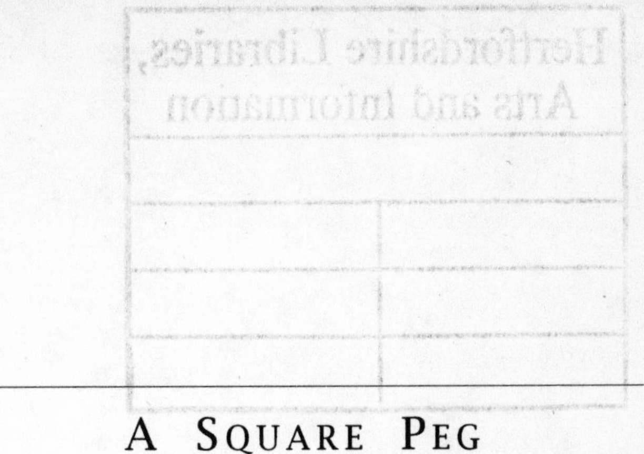

A Square Peg

An Ulster Childhood

Elizabeth McCullough

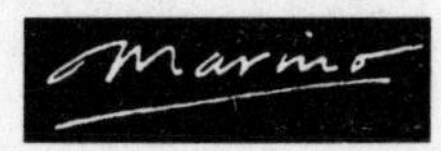

First published in 1997 by
Marino Books
16 Hume Street Dublin 2

Trade enquiries to CMD Distribution
55A Spruce Ave Stillorgan Industrial Park
Blackrock County Dublin

ISBN 1 86023 065 2

10 9 8 7 6 5 4 3 2 1

A CIP record for this title is available from the British Library

Cover and inside photos courtesy of the author
Cover design by Penhouse Design Group
Set by Richard Parfrey
Printed in Ireland by ColourBooks
Baldoyle Industrial Estate Dublin 13

Published in the US and Canada by the Irish American Book Company, 6309 Monarch Park Place, Niwot, Colorado, 80503
Tel: (303) 530-1352, (800) 452-7115
Fax: (303) 530-4488, (800) 401-9705

For A. S. who over the years encouraged
in his inimitable way
and in loving memory of my mother and San

ACKNOWLEDGEMENTS

Thanks are due to my daughter Katharine, who let me loose on her PC and printer; Business Base, Haddington; Margaret Beveridge and Maureen Fantom, who helped me towards some basic competence thereon; and my son Michael who came to the rescue in the final stages of editing on the screen; Marion Robertson who, by reading early drafts, encouraged me to persevere; Pyramid Photographic Laboratory in Edinburgh, which did such a good job on the reproductions; and staff at the Inishowen Maritime Heritage Co Ltd, Greencastle, County Donegal, who helped me find Drumaweir House.

Contents

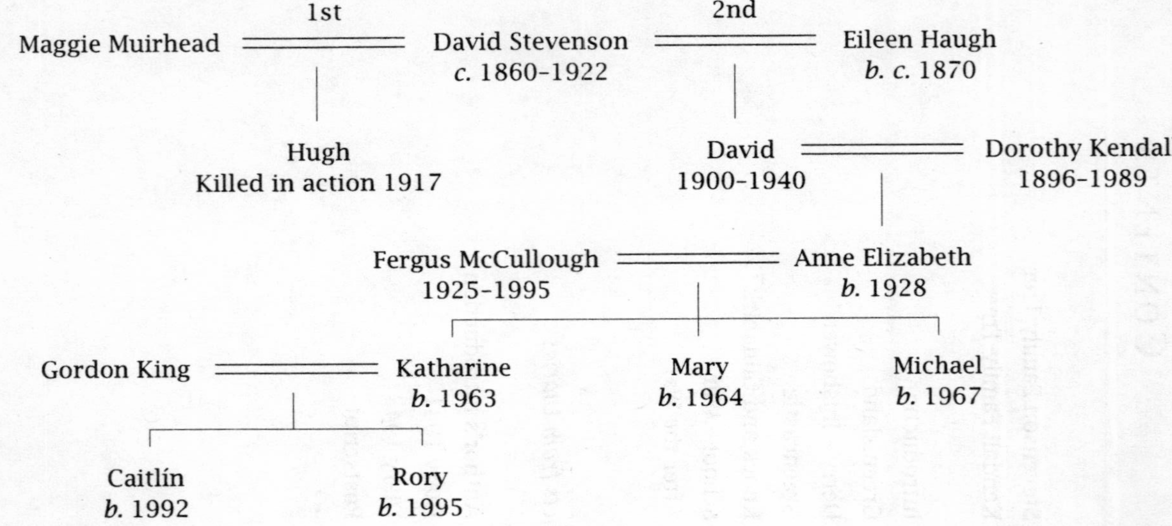
1st
Maggie Muirhead
David Stevenson
c. 1860–1922
2nd
Eileen Haugh
b. c. 1870
Hugh
Killed in action 1917
David
1900–1940
Dorothy Kendall
1896–1989
Fergus McCullough
1925–1995
Anne Elizabeth
b. 1928
Gordon King
Katharine
b. 1963
Mary
b. 1964
Michael
b. 1967
Caitlín
b. 1992
Rory
b. 1995

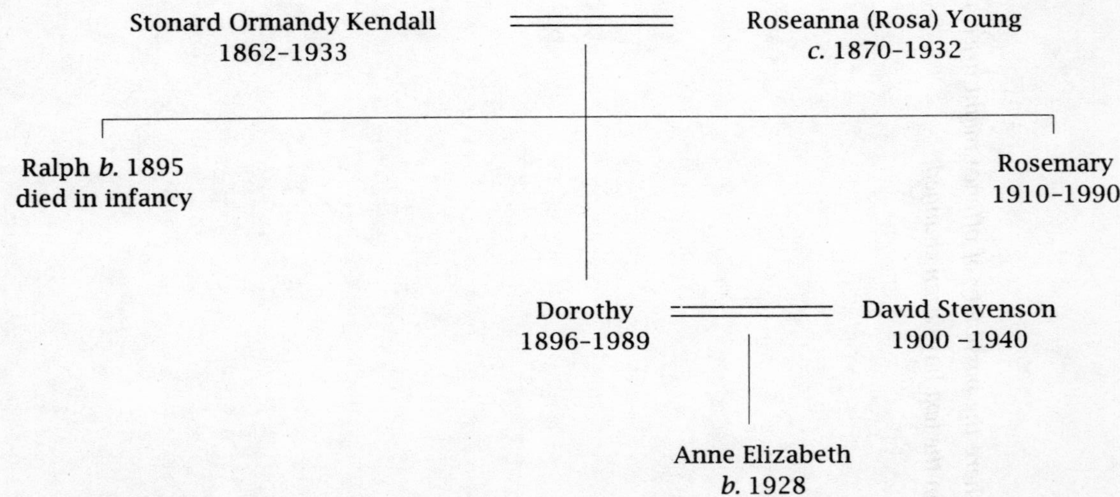
Stonard Ormandy Kendall
1862–1933
Roseanna (Rosa) Young
c. 1870–1932
Ralph b. 1895
died in infancy
Rosemary
1910–1990
Dorothy
1896–1989
David Stevenson
1900 –1940
Anne Elizabeth
b. 1928

Note: Where the possibility of offence might arise, certain names in the text have been changed.

INTRODUCTION

When I began about five years ago to write what has turned into the current work, it was my intention to write neither an autobiography nor a celebration of a familial centenary. Forces or voices beyond my control took over, however, and what started as a few vignettes of memorable characters from childhood, turned into *A Square Peg*. Sad circumstances forced me to set aside the original notes and in the intervening period I discovered my entire diaries for 1941 and 1948: much of their content is trivial but they display an honesty about what was going on in my very limited world; they also record entertaining glimpses of some of the characters mentioned in the main text.

At the time of writing this introduction, which I find to be the most difficult part of the whole thing, my mother would have been approaching her hundredth birthday – she was born on 29 November 1896. One of the most remarkable photographs I have unearthed must be that taken just after her birth: it shows her young mother (Rosa), grandmother and great-grandmother, who must even at a conservative estimate have been born around 1830, allowing twenty-five years to a generation. Our family married progressively later in life and bore children at what must then have been considered an almost indecent time of life, so my estimate is not exaggerated.

Why has an introduction been the most difficult part to write? There must be some sort of guilt factor at work:

if so, it is a fairly recent phenomenon which may well have been triggered by reading two autobiographical books written by authors respectively nine and seven years older than I: *The Railway Man* by Eric Lomax and *Cleared for Take-Off* by Dirk Bogarde, which recount their vastly different, although in many ways similar, experiences of the horrors of the Second World War. My reading of these has made me accept that there is no credible excuse for non-involvement in a conflict between what is patently evil and the variety of systems operating under the umbrella of democracy. I can no longer condemn entirely the use of non-nuclear forces, as I am convinced that we are rapidly approaching total destruction of the human habitat and, as my husband used to emphasise, as soon as an animal's habitat is under serious threat, extinction of the species is merely a matter of time.

For the first time I have come to realise just how critical was the exact year of one's birth between the two wars. Born in 1919, if male, one was just ripe for slaughter by 1939; born in 1921, one still qualified on leaving school to submit one's hard won credentials for disposal in some way thought useful to King and Country. Born in 1928, as I was, unless miserably evacuated to some place distant from parents and home, existence was relatively carefree, and one's concept of what was going on in the insane world limited, unless, of course, one had a father on active service. Even that worry did not impinge upon me, as my father had opted out of any rewarding life, and would in any case have been too old at thirty-nine. He had joined the army at the age of sixteen without his parents' knowledge, but my determined grandmother's intervention ensured that he had an income to supplement his army pay and never saw active service in France, where his half-brother perished in 1917.

I am well aware that my feelings of guilt at having passed the war years and those just after in a frivolous manner, largely preoccupied with clothes, cinema and sports, are somewhat irrational. This is, however, the way it was for me, and the feelings are a necessary part of the journey towards some sort of maturity.

My mother's early life was deeply affected by the insanity of European politics. On leaving school in 1914, instead of pursuing the usual female skills of the time – needlework, watercolour painting, piano playing – she went to work on a conveyor belt, making shellcases in Mackie's Foundry.

Seemingly some sort of social life continued throughout that war, as diaries record trips to Greencastle in County Donegal, where the family had spent holidays since 1910. The involvement of the United States of America in 1917 brought an infusion of young officers to enliven the scene, and weekend festivities continued throughout that terrible time, during which my mother became engaged to a young officer from Belfast who perished just four days before the armistice was signed. These experiences, however, did not alter her belief that all young men should sacrifice themselves for the current ideal, and by the end of the 1939–45 war, when I had begun to attract a following of young men, I was always fearful that they might not measure up to her requirements if they were even one year older than I. Eighteen years old and they would have been conscripted in mainland UK, but in Northern Ireland – and indeed the Republic – the right thing to do, in her mind and that of most others of our class, was to volunteer for service. Already vague thoughts had floated to the top of the confused soup which constituted my superficial philosophy of life, that conscientious objection might be an attitude to admire, rather than something to be condemned.

The decade 1950–60 was spent in a marriage doomed to failure from its irresponsible start. I remember saying blithely that I had no intention of having children, and that if it did not work we could always get a divorce. It took almost exactly a decade gate to gate.

There were many years during which I harboured feelings of resentment towards my mother for imagined omissions or commissions in her rearing of a sole, unwanted child. Now I can see that she did her best according to her own somewhat Edwardian standards, and in very difficult financial and emotional circumstances. Unlike Philip Larkin I do not believe that, 'They fuck you up, your mum and dad'. They may have been less than helpful at times, but the ultimate choices (extreme cases excepted) lie with the child.

In 1960 I finally began to get things right, resigned from an interesting job and sailed to West Africa to join the man I had met in 1955 and profoundly loved throughout our forty years together. Thereafter we lived in both West and East Africa, in the USA, and for the last twenty years in France; but only intermittently, when on home leave, in Ireland.

1
Greenisland

My parents' miserable six-year marriage effectively ended, not in a clean-cut divorce, but in what was at the time deemed more socially acceptable, an informal separation, just four months after my birth. My father came to inspect 'the fruit of his loins', remarked that it was a pity it was not a male and went out to celebrate with his ever-available drinking companions. Apparently an abundant supply of milk could have been supplied by 'nature's founts' but these rapidly dried up due to the unrelenting stress prevailing at a time which, in any normal family, would have been a time of joy. It seems my early days were troubled by colic while the resident nurse tried a number of unsuitable powdered products on the infant. Three weeks after the obligatory time spent flat in bed, my mother resumed her customary life of riding and gardening, but had also to organise the evacuation of our mock-Tudor mansion at Shantallow on the outskirts of Derry. Without prior consultation my father sold her favourite hunter Nimrod to a local woman renowned for having a 'hard hand on the bit'. I suspect this was the cruellest decision he ever made involving my mother because, when reminiscing, she always referred sooner or later to the deed. The sundry employees, including cook, house-parlourmaid, chauffeur and gardener/handyman, were paid off and the fox-terriers sold. It must also have been very painful for my mother to abandon the beautiful garden she had created during her six years in Derry.

The next five years were spent in my maternal grandparents' house at Greenisland on the shores of Belfast Lough. Grandfather Stonard, his wife Rosa and my mother's much younger sister Rosemary had moved there on his retirement as Lloyd's surveyor at the Harland & Wolff shipyards in Belfast. His first appointment had been in 1910 to oversee the work on the *Titanic* and the family never left Ulster thereafter.

The house was a large, forbidding, late-Victorian cube, smoothly stuccoed and dark grey: its austerity, however, was redeemed by the site. A gravel drive swept from the Belfast-Carrickfergus road to the front of the house and right to the edge of the sea, from which the property was protected by a stone wall. A narrow gap with steep, green slime-covered stone steps, led down to the shingle and the then clear water of Belfast Lough. For a small child the foreshore was forbidden territory, and strangely enough this was a rule I never defied, even when strongly tempted to try to recover a much-loved articulated snake which one of my aunt's admirers had wittily contrived to throw over the wall. There were plaster urns on each side of the wide steps which led to the front porch, but all was grey and gravel apart from a few veronica and fuchsia bushes, the orchard and tennis court on the Belfast side, the vegetable plot and 'motor-house' on the Carrick side. 'Motor-house' was a term, along with 'wireless', to which my mother clung till teenage mockery finally persuaded her to adopt garage and radio instead. At the rear another wall and some trees screened us from the main road. To my child's eye, the small hill surmounted by Knockagh monument dominated everything. Clear in memory is the day my grandfather decided to drive us to the summit in his dark green Singer, which had a canvas top and carried its spare wheel on the dickey. An aura of female apprehension pervaded the car. Changing gear was not Gramp's forte, and he never fully mastered the art of double-declutching. A sweet-natured man, his usual expression of exasperation was 'bother', but he was on record as once having been so provoked as to exclaim 'damnation'.

My earliest memory is of being put outside in a beige pram, the sides of which were embossed in a vaguely Art Nouveau design with a turquoise blue lozenge in the centre of the scrolls, to benefit from the excoriating air which blew off the lough. During summer months a cream silk canopy with a fringe was optimistically substituted for the more weather-resistant hood. It was said that on being discovered slightly moist underneath, I had the cleverness to hazard that it must have been raining. Only in late life has it occurred to me that my pressing need to be near open sea, albeit neither in nor on it, may stem from those first memories of waves lapping the shingle and gulls waiting on the sea wall for whatever scraps might come their way.

Helping my grandfather mark the tennis court with a lime-filled roller was another highlight of those early days, although there were inevitable injunctions not to get in the way, or touch the corrosive mixture. There was a gnarled apple tree with a deep, dankly smelling hole resembling an Edmund Dulac illustration. This hole was seemingly bottomless and sinister. A green glass fishing float was suspended in a net from the branches above. A hammock, into which I never managed to clamber successfully, linked this tree to a neighbouring one. My grandmother, despite her air of fragility, could manage it and would recline there, long skirts elegantly draped, silk parasol nearby.

There were tennis parties, and I remember the heavy oval rackets with bare wooden incised handles which were much more satisfying to flourish than my own red metal and string model. In the kitchen much of the morning would be devoted to sandwich preparation: mountains of brown cucumber triangles with all the crust neatly trimmed off, and equal quantities of white ones filled with egg and cress, piled up to be kept fresh under damp tea-towels till the afternoon.

Last minute panic prevailed before everyone was approved as being suitably dressed to meet the guests. Annie, our maid, also had to change from her lavender and white cotton morning uniform to black crêpe with a white cap and apron. Those females young enough to play tennis wore the dreary pleated skirts of the period; the men wore heavy, cream-coloured, full-length flannel trousers. My grandfather always wore his Panama hat, while my grandmother would circulate twirling her delicate cream silk parasol with its lace-trimmed edges and corded silk toggle. Little caps with shiny green visors, such as now favoured by Jim Courier, were worn by both sexes.

The kitchen was a magnet and I adored spending time with Annie, watching her making little chequered butterballs with the aid of two wooden pats; the balls were then put to float in a bowl of cold water till needed. Sometimes, even more satisfyingly, the butter could be packed into a wooden mould from which it was forced out bearing the imprint of a cow or flowers.

Much of Annie's work related to the endless laundry, so I could enjoy her company in the Turkish-bath atmosphere, till my grandmother inevitably appeared with admonitions about getting in the way and keeping Annie back from her work. Oddly misshapen lumps of starch had to be ground to a paste, to which was added the tincture from a tightly bound little blue cotton bag. Then there was the mangling, done by an enormous, almost industrial-sized, piece of machinery that lurked somewhere in the steamy, wool-smelling fog of the laundry room. Even blankets were sometimes washed, folded and then persuaded through the heavy rollers. I do not remember Annie having any help with manhandling those unwieldy wads, which had then to be hoisted to dry on ceiling-height rails, or occasionally hung outside to sweeten in the sharp wind. Clothes pegs were of the Beatrix Potter sort – wooden, with a knob at the top and two legs, quite impractical and often failing in their duty. There were literally hundreds of handkerchiefs which had to be twice-boiled. The texture of the brew at the end of the first boiling made it clear why a second was necessary. Gramp suffered from chronic catarrh, and Kleenex, had it existed then, would surely have been regarded as a luxury. Yellowish bar soap was used for most of the wash, but I think Lux flakes were used for finer items. Ironing, then as now, was an unappealing occupation, so I abandoned Annie when it came to that.

Strangely enough I do not remember any food preparation other than the making of sandwiches and cakes, although we always had a traditional Sunday luncheon of roast beef, Yorkshire pudding, criminally over-cooked vegetables, as well as roast and boiled potatoes. Puddings were steamed and heavy. These meals were a mixed pleasure, as it was held that too much meat was bad for children. I adored the pink bits, whether lamb or beef. However, ostensibly for reasons of health, it was strictly rationed and my otherwise kindly grandfather called me a 'meat-hog'. Manners were to be minded, implements held correctly, and certainly no elbow ever rested on the table. Children were to be seen and not heard, so from a very early age I was attuned to sitting in on adult conversations. There was the consolation of my high-rimmed plate with a picture of golf-playing teddy bears on the bottom, although another frequent exhortation to me was to leave the pattern on the plate. Felix the Cat was beautifully satin-stitched on my favourite bib, and I can remember in detail his rounded red tongue, wild eyes and fine whiskers, as well as the blue scalloped edge of the white linen. Mass production had not yet standardised all items relating to child-care, the age of ubiquitous plastic being still distant, although we did have Bakelite picnic mugs and pencil boxes.

Women spent many hours making useless things such as traycloths, embroidered pictures of olde English thatched cottages and gardens, and samplers. The darkly curtained drawing room was filled with examples of female industry in the form of bell-pulls, firescreens and little beaded purses. It must have been in this room that Gramp had his world globe, with the aid of which, a ping-pong ball and a torch, he would spend long sessions trying to describe the workings of the solar system to me. He must have been not far from death, but his patience was infinite and I remain grateful to this day, as his explanations made early geography lessons a comparative walkover. Our sundial on the other hand totally confused me, although I pretended to understand.

I was precociously fashion conscious and did not at all appreciate the Viyella drop-waisted dresses my mother made and embroidered with the same stylised design of daisies she later painted on a silver frieze above the tile level in our bathroom. Her explanation for clinging to the style of the 1920s was that children had no waist, and straight up and down suited the infant form much better. Auntie Rosemary contributed to this collection by knitting or crocheting further models in fine blue wool streaked with silver-grey thread. I remember with some pain being asked to hold a skein of this wool for winding into a ball and incurring her wrath by dropping the lot in a tangled mess. Not long after this my fashion ideal became Shirley Temple, with ringlets, ankle-strap shoes and a frilly waisted dress with a large satin bow at the rear. Ringlets were regarded, with some justification, as being distinctly lower class. I was told they were produced by wrapping the hair in newspaper: indeed one sometimes saw grubby children out on the streets of Whiteabbey wearing such wrappings as they whipped little wooden tops and played hopscotch among the wriggly chalk markings on the pavements.

Ankle-strap shoes were also out on the grounds of their implicit vulgarity and because they were bad for your feet. So I remained straight of hair and dress, wearing sensible shoes with a bar across the instep and, worst of all, a button to fasten them. Several years later, by dint of much pleading, I graduated to a slip-on style with buckles, although these too were suspected of being potential foot-deformers. For parties (of which there were few and I hated them, having already begun to feel a loner, not knowing what to say to other children) bronze Kate Greenaway slippers with crossover elastic were permitted. One of Gramp's preoccupations was roughening the soles of new party shoes, and this was done with a file in his large, draughty workshop at the far end of the 'motor-house'. Dressing up for children's parties remained a serious business till the outbreak of war and the introduction of clothes rationing. A dark blue velvet dress with a lace collar and cut steel buttons down the front was my outfit: in winter a blue velvet cloak with a high ruched collar completed the ensemble. Rarely did the parties get out of hand to the extent that escape to the shrubberies outside was permitted. For the most part the games were musical chairs, naming the items on a tray, and hide-and-seek in those turn of the century houses which provided so many satisfying understair cupboards, attic rooms and tables draped with heavy bobble-fringed green chenille covers.

Gramp thought, quite correctly, that my mother was neglectful in terms of spiritual guidance, and did his best with illustrated Bible stories. With shame I recall being unresponsive to the tales of the infant Samuel, Moses in the bulrushes and Joseph's 'bloody little coat' – an expression my mother had used in her own childhood to the horror of the adults – wriggling to escape from Gramp's restraining grip and pleading for Peter Rabbit or Benjamin Bunny instead. Even *Tanglewood Tales* or *The Water Babies* were preferable to the Bible stories.

Force-fed, I early developed a loathing of the Greek myths. In them, however, a latent tendency to voyeurism got off to a good start: the Gorgon's head of writhing serpents, the one-eyed Cyclops, Europa and the bull, Icarus plunging earthwards, all had a certain compelling attraction. I must have been twelve before I could summon enough courage to look at the picture of the Cyclops trying to find Ulysses. I liked thumbing with great care through Auntie Rosemary's copy of *The Ancient Mariner*, illustrated by Edmund Dulac, each plate protected by a thin tissue. Deep respect for books was early instilled and I would never have contemplated 'improving' illustrations or turning down corners to mark the place. These were regarded, together with licking one's finger to turn the page, as being essentially proletarian habits.

My mother, whose relationship with her sister younger by thirteen years remained a guarded one throughout their long lives, used to show me, as horrible examples of book desecration, turn of the century copies of Andrew Lang's fairy tales which Auntie Rosemary had embellished with crimson lake, yellow-ochre (where she felt gold was called for) and Prussian blue. There was no sign then of her talent for art, so I was suitably impressed by the heinous nature of the crime. *Peter Rabbit*, *The Tale of Two Bad Mice* and *Squirrel Nutkin* remained my favourites till displaced by *Black Beauty*, *What Katy Did*, *Little Women*, the William books, nearly all the E. Nesbit stories and, ultimately, Bulldog Drummond, with whom – as well as Peter Wimsey – I fell in love at the age of about ten. I returned again and again to *Ruthless Rhymes for Heartless Homes* and Belloc's *Cautionary Tales*, so aptly illustrated by Bentley. Professor Branestawm, with the ingenious drawings of Heath Robinson, also kept me engrossed for hours on end. Comics were predictably forbidden, although eventually Mickey Mouse annuals and illustrated versions of the Disney 'Silly Symphonies' were permitted. Nature study was neglected, and I suspect none of the grown-ups knew much about wildlife, although Gramp did have books on the identification of birds, butterflies and fishes.

Memories of my grandmother, Rosa, whose face so sweetly smiles from photographs, are fainter and without affection. Admonition and restraint from following one's impulses were what I associated with her. I was also vaguely aware of her advice to my mother that: 'You will have to take a strong line with that one.' Whether this was reported to me at a later date as something of a joke or, as I recall it, in the bathroom where I had loudly complained about the bath's scratchy, bottom-searing enamel, I cannot be certain. The scene, however, remains vivid: my grandmother bending over the bath, lathering me with Pears Golden Glory soap, when my mother joined us. The bath had lion's claw feet and there was a massive watercloset with blue flowers in the bowl and a wide wooden seat. The upper part of the bathroom door out to the landing was glazed with star-spangled panes of glass in the same vibrant colours as those favoured by Auntie Rosemary in her book embellishments, except the blue was royal rather than Prussian. I remember also praying fervently that my grandmother would not feel prompted, as my mother was from time to time, to clean out my navel with a sharp fingernail. I used to implore her to desist as the sensation seemed life-threatening and even now I cannot bear to explore the cavity.

Christmas 1932 was the last one when both grandparents were still alive. I shared a room with my mother, from which Auntie Rosemary had been evicted with understandable resentment to an attic room next to Annie's. The wardrobe had two small stained-glass windows of Art Nouveau design, backed with green gathered fabric – quite useless, but so decorative that my love of Art Nouveau probably stems from that time. I used to sit inside the wardrobe with the door almost closed, watching the filtered light that shone dimly through the green curtained glass. I remember waking on Christmas Day, to fissle through the big blue cotton sack that had been hung the night before at the end of the bed. There was a bracelet of tiny pearls from which hung a blue glass elephant: I think this was a gift from Auntie Rosemary, and I got the impression it was slightly disapproved of as being 'jewellery' and therefore unsuitable for children; an articulated green-marbled papier-mâché snake (the one that ended its days on the shingle below our sea wall) with a bright red tongue; a small box of building blocks; and the traditional tangerine wrapped in silver paper. The main present, a red wooden-seated tricycle, was too big for the sack, and stood at the bottom of the bed. The tricycle caused trouble almost as soon as it was taken downstairs, as the only place where one could get up any speed was in the hall leading from the kitchen to the dining room. Rosa's displeasure was manifest as she and Auntie Rosemary prepared the Christmas table setting; Rosa had only a few weeks to live, dying almost exactly a year before my grandfather.

A resident nurse had been engaged for the last months of Gramp's illness, so my perambulations around the house became increasingly solitary, as he was confined to his room and the other adults were understandably pre-occupied. Around this time my imagination was first stimulated by talk of the Loch Ness monster. Many of my drawings were devoted to impressions of it and of the nurse, whose headgear I both admired and envied. There are painful memories of sessions in the sick-room, to which my mother brought me to demonstrate my precocity in reading, which was genuine, and my advancement in numbers, which was nil. For some reason a mental block set in after the naming of the number five, and I was taken out in tearful shame, my mother hissing that I *must* remember it. I repeated much the same heartless exercise with my own innumerate daughters forty years later.

There were undoubtedly musical genes on Rosa's side of the family: one of her sisters had played first violin with the Newcastle-upon-Tyne Symphony Orchestra, and two extrovert brothers had been Gilbert & Sullivan enthusiasts. Both my mother and aunt were quite proficient pianists, although there was a marked difference in their touch. My mother used to wince and make sibilant noises while Rosemary hammered out Sinding's 'Rustle of Spring': 'More like a tornado.' Secretly I admired her skill, and enjoyed her aggressive renditions of various *marches militaires*, and such of Lizst's Hungarian rhapsodies as she could assault with any degree of competence. My own taste evolved during the 1930s to favour the heavily sentimental or violently dramatic. I adored Grieg's *Peer Gynt* Suite and Tchaikovsky's 1812 Overture. I was, however, equally happy with Sousa's marches or Nelson Eddy and Jeanette MacDonald singing 'I'll See You Again'. I was deprived of Bach because my mother did not empathise with him. As it was generally agreed that I was tone deaf and devoid of any sense of rhythm, no money was wasted on formal teaching. More probably I was inhibited by self-consciousness, not to mention unrelenting adverse criticism. I spent much time trying to work out musical scores on our short keyboard piano, but with little success.

Another theory put about was: 'She doesn't like dolls.' Actually, I had no strong feelings for or against dolls but got the impression that to display much interest in them would not go down well. This despite the fact that Gramp had made a beautiful miniature rocking cradle to hold a doll of no more than nine inches long. I used to put miniature teddy bears to bed in it. Maybe the grandparents and my mother had subconsciously wanted a male child to replace my mother's older brother, who was 'blue' and lived only a few months, dying in 1895. (I recently found the letters which firstly congratulate Rosa and Stonard on the infant's birth, then sadly, about four months later, offer condolence on his death.) Whatever the reason, Meccano sets at Christmas, with birthday additions thereto, Hornby trains, building blocks and chemistry sets were to be my lot throughout childhood.

The violin-playing sister of Rosa has gone down in family history as 'Auntie-Gertie-who-ran-away'. The reasons for Gertie's decampment will never be known, but it apparently 'broke her father's heart', as she had been not only the most beautiful but also undeniably his favourite daughter. My mother remembered being about six years old and present in an attic room in Newcastle-upon-Tyne while furious rows took place between Gertie and Josephine, the eldest of the sisters. One of these rows seems to have preceded what was a midnight flit. One can only conjecture an affair with a member of the orchestra, pregnancy or both. She was never heard of again.

We had a telephone hung on the wall with a wind-up mechanism and an earpiece which had to be unhooked, but it was infrequently used. Gramp also had one of those classic gramophones with a huge trumpet on top and the HMV fox-terrier on the central label of all the records. I cannot recall anything of his musical taste but I do clearly remember him pottering around his workshop humming, 'Pom-tiddly-pom-pom, pom-*pom*', and he encouraged me to listen to his conch shell from the Indian Ocean.

As for musical or literary tastes and talents on the paternal side of my family, it seems that my father's favourite song was 'When Father Painted the Parlour'. This is probably apocryphal, as my mother liked to give the impression that he was a philistine in all matters of art, music and literature and had even proven ineducable when sent as a last resort to Sedbergh, a public school in Cumbria. *His* father, on the other hand, left a library of well-read, leather-bound volumes of nineteenth-century literature, including works of most of the major poets. The males on the Derry side of the family cannot *all* have devoted their time exclusively to the acquisition of money, shooting and the breeding of fox-terriers, as my mother would have had it.

Predictably Josephine (in future referred to as Auntie Jo) drifted into the classic role of spinster who stays at home to look after aging parents. There had been a fourth sister, Phyllis, born when my great-grandmother was in middle age, who spent her fourteen years' existence in a wheelchair. What her disability was I do not know, but my mother said she looked normal enough.

After the deaths of great-grandmother Young and Phyllis, Auntie Jo and her father moved to Torquay, where they remained until his death in the late 1920s. Letters I unearthed recently reveal his preoccupation with continuance of the family line and regret that there was no male issue. Auntie Jo's subsequent near pauperism would indicate that all the family capital was exhausted during those final years. She returned to Newcastle-upon-Tyne and survived till just after the Second World War, leading a solitary existence in a small flat, and making occasional day-trips to Robin Hood's Bay and Whitby. I never met her but had to write a dutiful card at Christmas, and thank-you notes afterwards for the half-crown book token which was her unvarying gift. The writing of thank-you letters on

Boxing Day was a discipline ruthlessly imposed which threw a cloud on that day throughout most of my childhood. There was no hope of delaying the job nor any chance to exercise childish spontaneity; each note had to be word-perfect, correctly punctuated and devoid of erasure. Many tear-stained efforts ended up in the wastepaper basket.

Auntie Jo's countenance became grimmer as the years passed, and she was never able to purge herself of the grievance hatched at the time of my mother's marriage in 1922, when she felt slighted at being booked into the Royal Avenue Hotel in Belfast, rather than staying in the already full family house in Adelaide Park. She was terrified that republican violence might erupt at any time, and wrote a most unkind letter to Gramp after the wedding. Notwithstanding his hurt, he continued to give her financial support throughout his life. My mother and Auntie Rosemary also supplemented her pension from their own meagre funds during the late 1930s and throughout the war until her death.

The musical uncles disappeared from the scene, unmarried and seemingly without having made any worthwhile contribution to the family business. From my mother I got the impression that the firm failed for much the same reasons that later led to the sale of the Derry bakery and restaurant: dissipated young men at the helm, who clocked in late and helped themselves freely to the cash to support their lifestyle. Drink was not mentioned in connection with the Newcastle uncles but my mother recalled that: 'The uncles were always jolly.' One wonders.

Spontaneous tactile display of affection did not exist

in our family any more than did the use of names, 'you' being deemed sufficient. My mother always called Rosa 'Mother', although until she died she always referred to Gramp as 'Daddy'. I do not remember ever being hugged or comforted, and the only knees I ever sat upon were those of Gramp and Auntie Judy who lived in Lurgan. Ritual pecks were exchanged in greeting and one was kissed 'Goodnight' after having gabbled, 'Gentle Jesus, meek and mild', presumably at the behest of Gramp: this habit did not endure long after my mother and I moved to Knock and Gilnahirk many miles away in County Down. What came after 'Pity me a little child' is a blank.

Auntie Judy was not a real aunt; indeed I don't know how my mother became friendly with her. Later I heard a rumour that she was the illegitimate fruit of the loins of some minor member of the aristocracy. She was very fond of me and left a small legacy when she died. We used to drive down to Lurgan for afternoon tea several times a year, but I had mixed feelings about these trips, as there was neither toy nor animal in Auntie Judy's house to enliven the afternoon. There was a glass dome filled with tiny stuffed tropical birds, a vastly complicated brass clock, also housed under a glass dome on the chimney piece, on each side of which was a pair of useless ornaments from which hung dangling crystals of dark blue cut glass.

Judy was cushiony, with soft pink and white skin and fine snow-white hair tightly drawn back into a bun, and she never changed her Edwardian style of dress. Her blouses were high-necked, made of finely pleated black silk, sometimes embroidered with tiny jet beads. Below the blouse she wore an ankle-length black or charcoal-coloured heavy serge skirt. She loved to clasp me to her ample frontage which ran in a steep slope towards the floor, so there was not really any knee on which to perch, and inevitably I wriggled. Auntie Judy's cake stand was the best stocked I can remember: minute wafer-thin, moist white bread sandwiches filled with ham or egg and cress, brown ones with fish paste, buttered and jammed scones, pink sugar-coated biscuits with little white figures, cream buns, sometimes a cream-filled sponge cake, and occasionally the dreaded emetic caraway-seed variety. I adored the sugary biscuits and the cream buns but my mother regarded them with apprehension, fearing a subsequent 'bilious attack'. There was an ongoing, albeit amiable, battle between her and Auntie Judy, who always argued that just one more could surely do no harm. Sometimes I would be sick on the way home and would suffer, in consequence, a few days of particularly spartan meals.

One visit ended sadly. Judy had a unique way of hoisting her considerable weight from one step of the stairs to the next and I had followed behind, imitating her style. I do not imagine she saw, and I certainly did not do it in any disrespectful sense, merely thinking it an entertaining method of getting upstairs. Anyhow, after the initial pronouncement from my mother that the incident would be fully discussed later and suitable punishment meted out when we got home, a grim silence set in for the homeward drive. I was miserable because I could not understand what it was all about. I was spanked and sent straight to bed to ponder my misdeed. Future visits were therefore always clouded with the thought that I might unwittingly commit some further transgression and be punished accordingly.

The most severe punishment ever inflicted was the result of my having 'struck my parent'. In my mother's view – and she undoubtedly got this from her own parents – it was the worst sin a child could commit. We had been on a rare trip to the shoreline, somewhere down the Ards peninsula, and on the journey home I must have done something in the back of the car to provoke a slap from the driver's seat. Purely in reflex, I slapped back. That incident resulted in my being 'sent to Coventry' for a four-day stretch; when it was grimly explained that total silence was to prevail over that period I was devastated. Far from repenting my sins, I sat in my room vowing vengeance and sticking my tongue out in whatever direction I hoped might most deeply penetrate my mother. Psychologically I was broken long before the four-day period was up, and my howls did bring about a diminished sentence.

Another memory of that time is of being taken out to see the Graf Zeppelin, which was floating in the sky somewhere near the Sydenham docks. I have a suspicion that I did not actually spot it but pretended to have done so. We also went to watch the annual TT races on the road between Dundonald and Newtownards, and sometimes had a spectacular view from Flo's house in the main square of Comber of those smelly, noisy vehicles negotiating the bend to take them back towards Newtownards. (Flo appears in the 1941 diary – a super horsewoman.) There was a choking atmosphere and even then I felt repugnance and apprehension at the risks taken by the drivers. There were point-to-point races too, with the joy of being allowed to perch on a seat-stick and being near enough to the jockeys to appreciate the full glory of their garish satin tops. These trips must have taken place after my grandfather's death, or without his knowledge, as I know he would have disapproved of betting. Cards, however, were not prohibited and I recall Auntie Rosemary playing endless games of patience and making houses out of the entire pack. Gramp's attitudes were strictly Victorian, and my mother told of having been sent from the dining room after his exclamation, 'Dorothy, you have been painting again!' She swore it was merely a light dusting of papier poudré but I suspect there may well have been a touch of lipstick. The works of Oscar Wilde were not allowed in the house, but the reason for that remained a mystery to me until much later in life. My mother, when referring to the ban, was evasive as to why it had been imposed: 'Something he did with another man' was as far as I got.

There were travelling circuses of a disgustingly primitive nature: I remember being taken to a Duffy's tent just outside Killyleagh, bursting with anticipation of I had no idea what. Horses I was well accustomed to, although not ridden by plump females dressed in spangles and coiffed with ostrich plumes. There were sealions balancing multicoloured balls, and a bored-looking juvenile elephant which defecated not far from the barrier dividing the audience from the ring. We were seated very near the edge and became a target for the witticisms of the clown, who terrified me with his grotesque gloves and his too-close mouth of gigantic, threatening false teeth.

Very recently I unearthed some documents locked up in a small metal box, which give much insight into Gramp's formative years in Cumbria. They comprise an exchange of letters between him and his Uncle Willie, who was trustee of a then considerable fortune, something of the order of £30,000, which was to pass to Stonard (Gramp) on his attainment of majority. The tone changes from puzzled aggrievement on the part of my grandfather, to hurt evasion by Uncle Willie, to the outright confrontation which eventually brought about a grovelling admission of some culpability in the dissipation of Gramp's inheritance. Willie makes pathetic pleas of fatigue, having had to work late clarifying the accounts of the previous ten years, boils on the neck due to overwork, and a particularly unconvincing explanation as to how his bank had mislaid some critical figures. Nothing was ever recovered from the Antrim Pig Iron investments, nor did the negligent bank which had 'somehow' lost records, including Willie's bank book, ever come up with the figures. Stonard, a strictly honourable young man, with recently acquired family commitments, tied these letters up tightly and kept them in a little tin box, which seems not to have been opened till I did so, almost exactly one hundred years after the correspondence came to an end. Gramp must not have talked much about the lost fortune, or blackened the name of Willie, otherwise it would have filtered down to me, along with the details of other siblings and the emigration of his much older sister Polly to Australia. She, and her issue, slowly evaporated, leaving addresses written in increasingly laborious script, and from which ultimately no answer came.

In the tin box I found the engagement pictures of Stonard and Rosa, a lock of her hair and the tiny silver-edged invitation card announcing the date of their marriage in August 1893. Gramp's last few years must have been heavily clouded by the revelation that my mother's seemingly ideal marriage to a handsome young man of property who lived in Derry was a disastrous failure.

The telephone call telling my mother of Gramp's death came after we had moved to a small house he had built for her at the foot of the Gilnahirk hills on the outskirts of Belfast. That call, along with the death of her dog Michael, and the Chamberlain broadcast announcing that a state of war had been declared between Great Britain and Nazi Germany, are the only times I remember my mother crying.

2

DERRY – INISHOWEN

Not long after the death of my mother's parents, I became aware of having a third grandparent, Grandma Stevenson, who was to make a forceful impression on me, as she did on everyone with whom she came in contact or, more often, conflict. Many years were to pass before I began to get a glimmering of the savage emotional undercurrents which strained relations between her and my mother. Our early meetings were strictly formal, taking place in the Royal Avenue Hotel, where she always stayed during her visits to Belfast. At one of these it must have been arranged that my mother and I would pass an annual summer holiday as her guests at Drumaweir in Greencastle, County Donegal. The meetings must have been of the nature of 'access to the child' on a quarterly basis. The many misunderstandings between these two very determined women were largely resolved over the years, as they gradually discovered how my father had contrived to keep them apart, and had even provoked further ill-feeling by freely distorting the facts. For instance, he never revealed that the house he and my mother occupied remained the property of *his* mother: this to some extent explained her frequent, none-too-welcome, intrusive visits during the early days of their marriage, when she would demand of my very reticent mother if there was 'no sign of a little stranger yet?' By deliberately fanning the flames of suspicion, he ensured they would meet seldom and therefore be less likely to join forces in an effort to control his drinking.

Grandma (Eileen) Stevenson, Her Ladyship or Madam, as she was variously known, believed, in the ignorance which then, as now, cloaks the true nature of the disease of alcoholism, that 'the love of a good woman' and 'the pattering of little footsteps' would bring her wayward son to his senses. My mother had the misfortune to be cast in the role of the good woman, mine were the footsteps which eventually pattered.

I suspect that my conception after six years of childlessness was the result of what would now be termed 'rape within marriage'. In extreme old age, when my mother and I had reached a better understanding of, and respect for each other, I asked her if she had ever enjoyed sex. The sad reply was, 'Well, he was always drunk.' I suspect she was not in any case a highly-sexed animal, so she must have found few joys in the union. She devoted herself to horses, hunting and the garden, having little need to occupy herself with domestic affairs other than to decide the menus for the day. So, to outward appearances, this was an ideal union. The effort to keep Gramp and Rosa in ignorance of the true state of affairs reached ludicrous levels, and finally failed when Rosa was called upon to collect my unconscious father, who had been spending a night with 'the boys', from a pub in Cushendun. The Antrim coast road was not an easy drive in those days, and Rosa was not a confident driver: the experience was a humiliating one which she never forgot, much less forgave.

The two grandmothers had nothing in common except

the marriage of their offspring. Rosa considered Grandma Stevenson unladylike in her often uninhibited behaviour, loud Waterford brogue, and preference, never denied, for male company. Within the immediate family circle Madam was wholeheartedly disliked and feared, although it seems that my grandfather, David senior, remained a devoted slave who indulged her many whims till his death early in 1922. There were hysterical outbursts if she was frustrated in her schemes, at the end of which she would lie on the floor kicking and screaming, before retiring to bed exhausted, as was everyone else by the recriminations, announcing her intention to console herself with a hot toddy. There was general relief when she made herself scarce, which was seldom, as she was tireless in the delivery of unsolicited advice on all matters domestic, social, behavioural and educational.

In Derry she was renowned for what my mother witheringly called 'Your Grandma's Good Works'. She had undoubtedly 'made it' as a professional woman, having left Waterford in the late nineteenth century for nursing training at the Rotunda Hospital in Dublin, ultimately becoming matron of the Derry City hospital. She got an MBE for her work for the Soldiers' Sailors' and Airmen's Families Association, and is on record as having felt slighted that it was not an OBE or, better, a DBE. This may well be apocryphal, if one takes into account the bruised and generally outraged emotions of her immediate family, whose comments tended not to be notably charitable. On the incarceration of her sister in the Letterkenny Asylum, my father remarked that they had put the wrong one away.

She must have longed for posthumous recognition and admiration, to the extent that she left generous legacies of cash to a few well-connected, but certainly not needy persons. I am not clear how, if at all, these generous bequests were honoured, as her estate was virtually bankrupt at the time of her death in 1947. I, at one time described by her as going to be 'the richest young heiress in the northwest', inherited only my grandfather's vulgar horseshoe-shaped tie-pin, his signet ring – which I still wear – and a string of ill-matched pearls. Her diamond earrings went to a member of a titled family who was, I trust, suitably appreciative.

Grandma was an inveterate snob and name-dropper: a signed photograph of the Duchess of Abercorn was prominently on display in a silver frame in her sitting room, and she liked to refer to 'My dear friend, the duchess'. General Montgomery's mother, who lived at Moville on the Foyle, was also referred to as a dear friend, but my mother said the acquaintance probably amounted to no more than having sat on the same committee or platform.

After my grandfather died, Eileen observed all the ritual of full mourning, including the widow's veil. Thereafter, throughout her twenty-five years of widowhood, she never wore any colour other than black, grey, white or purple. Towards the end of her life the purple gene got out of hand, and she would order an entire 'costume' of the most expensive fine wool available in intense shades of violet, from 'dear Mr Dunn' who owned a tailoring business in Wellington Place in Belfast.

My birth, after six years of turbulent, childless,

marriage, was not the proverbial 'happy event'. Indeed it added further complication to a fraught state of affairs. It seems that a separation had already been agreed, so by the time I was four months old the domestic structure of the house on the outskirts of Derry had been dismantled. It was at that time, as I have said, that my mother and I went to live with her parents and sister on the shore of Belfast Lough. Thereafter my visits to Derry were infrequent and obviously stressful for my mother.

The drive from Belfast to Derry seemed interminable as we chuntered along in the Austin Seven, through Antrim, Toomebridge and ultimately over the Glenshane Pass, probably never exceeding forty miles an hour. Quite early in life I experienced a thrill when we got to the top of the Pass in the Sperrins, from which on a clear day one could see Errigal and Muckish in County Donegal. That view, and the delicate whiff of peat burning somewhere nearby, can still evoke a unique lightness of spirit.

Trips to Derry meant being indulged by various kind relatives, and a relaxation of the firm discipline imposed by Rosa. We stayed in Clarendon Street, on the steep slopes of which it was said that Madam had been toppled by some grudge-bearing acquaintance, who gave her trailing widow's veil a timely tug.

Cousin Ronald Cunningham ran his medical practice from Clarendon Street, and it was at their dining table that I first savoured the delight of Heinz tomato soup, which was offered in an attempt to soothe the raging sore throat I had hatched during the journey from Belfast. The house was tall, narrow and dark, and I do not remember much else about it except a sense of urgent coming and going – not surprising if he was running a general practice.

There were trips to the family bakery and restaurant, which were still functioning, although under a manager who held fifty-one per cent of the shares by this time. I was taken to the Dickensian office where the two Misses Steele were in charge of accounts: it was they whose arms had been regularly twisted for ready cash by the young boss (my father) and also by Her Ladyship.

At that time bread was delivered by horse-drawn van as far afield as County Donegal. I loved to visit the stables, which were immensely high, with motes of dust floating in the shafts of sunlight that filtered down from the high glazed roof. The shire horses were gentle and greedy for sugar lumps and carrots, and I loved to stroke their soft muzzles and ears. Thankfully nobody expected me to ride on them.

The Derry relatives were more expansive and spontaneous than my maternal ones: they were also free with gifts of crackers at Christmas, boxes of chocolate, Easter eggs and other indulgences, such as fireworks at Halloween. Cousin Norman McClure owned a bookshop and small publishing house in Shipquay Street and kept me supplied throughout childhood with a succession of ill-chosen books, till finally, possibly due to some hint from my mother, he changed to book tokens. He was very kind, but his imagination did not stretch beyond Angela Brazil's unquenchable output of girls' boarding-school stories, with which, of course, I could not identify. Norman's head was sharply domed, very pink, and highly polished. He had a number of large protuberant warts which fascinated me, as did his boy-scout pack-leader uniform, in which he sometimes visited us in Belfast. He was, notwithstanding, married to a lowland Scot, of whose Glaswegian accent my mother spoke disdainfully, and had two children somewhat older than me.

Even though I was often the centre of adult attention and relished that, I sometimes sensed pity, and was also perpetually aware of the chill relationship between my mother and Grandma Stevenson. The latter would take me off for a day, when permitted, in her battle-scarred car. In retrospect I can understand my mother's apprehension, as one of my earliest memories is of a noisy grating impingement as Grandma reversed out of a garage at Drumaweir Hotel. I think she managed to wrench the door-handle off one side of the car, which was, to make matters worse, a borrowed one.

Some years later we visited the city cemetery in Derry to lay flowers on 'dear Dave's grave'. Why she had to take the car right into the graveyard, I cannot imagine, but the back bumper got hooked onto one of the low-level chains surrounding someone else's plot, and there was a subsequent heated exchange with the sexton. That was one of the earliest incidents when I experienced the almost inevitable shame that resulted from being taken out for a 'treat' by Grandma. Embarrassment reached its peak during the war: stockings of any sort were in short supply, and she favoured finely ribbed silk-wool mixture ones – expensive at any time, as were most of her tastes. We went to a draper's shop in Portstewart, where she put one of her still shapely legs on the counter and demanded, 'Do you have any stockings like these, young man?' By this time I felt pinker than the young man looked, and needless to say he did not have any such. She could never be convinced that a cubicle in the ladies was genuinely occupied, and once even got down, head between legs, to verify the fact.

In Derry, at the height of the war, she decided to take me to the cinema to see an Abbot and Costello film. It was a dreary day, and there was a patient queue waiting for stalls and balcony on both sides of the entrance doors, which were clearly not going to be unlocked till the last sitting was due to be let out. She danced up and down, rattling the doors like a frustrated chimpanzee, till a puzzled commissionaire opened them and told her that, as she could see, there was queueing. She then asked if he was aware that she was 'Mrs David Stevenson of the Collon House'. This did not cut any ice, although he was not uncivil, merely remarking that that might well be the case, but she would just have to take her place 'like any other body'. Many amused eyes were riveted on the scene - a welcome diversion in the wet waiting period - but I wished the ground would swallow us both. Eventually, after we had endured whispered comments from others in the queue, the doors opened and we got seats in the balcony. Just in front of us were a sailor and his girlfriend, who were so entwined as to impede Grandma's view of the screen: she began by making loud comments; these having no effect, she prodded them apart with her umbrella. He did not turn round and punch her; they separated for a while, only to fuse again well before the end of the film.

'Uninhibited' and 'impetuous' were the adjectives most often used by my mother to describe Grandma's behaviour. She was stigmatised as having 'no reticence', as she would hurriedly exit from the lavatory still adjusting her clothes. This sort of incident was particularly shocking to both Rosa and my mother, who tried not to let themselves be seen entering a bathroom, much less exiting to the sound of rushing water. In the mid-1930s, when Mr Boyd, our weekly gardener, came for the day, my mother suffered because of the proximity to the lavatory window of the water-butt, from which he often drew water. She used to leave the tap running in the hand basin while she was inside, to disguise any inappropriate noises. What Mr Boyd did to relieve any call of nature I do not know, but I certainly never surprised him at an awkward moment.

Church attendance was another bone of contention, because Grandma felt, as had Gramp, that my education in terms of spiritual guidance and religious observance, was being utterly neglected. She had to negotiate permission to take me to a service, and my mother would try to put the onus of choice on me. As I had no idea what I was choosing, it seemed safe enough to give it a try and not offend Grandma. There were many aspects of being with her I did enjoy but I was inhibited from showing any enthusiasm for fear of arousing my mother's displeasure. Church attendances were few, as the excuse that I had 'a slight sniffle which might turn into a cold' was often used; as I was seldom without a sniffle, cough or wheeze, Grandma's triumphs were rare. She enjoyed the hymns and sang resonantly, if tunelessly, exhorting me between breaths to join in. I agonised about when to stand up, sit down, kneel or bow my head, and whether or not it was necessary to shut one's eyes in prayer. Finding the right place in the hymnal was also a worry and, seeing this, Grandma would make a noisy, page-rustling intervention, attracting, or so I felt, even more attention to our already noisy pew. To the mightiness of the organ, the beauty of the flowers or the colours of the stained glass, I was deaf and blind. Desire to escape and the fervent hope that she would not stop on the way out to present me to the reverend or some fellow worshipper, were uppermost in my mind.

Neglect of the religious side of my education did, however, have some positive benefits. I was incurious about other people's persuasion, oblivious of religious divides within our community, and without prejudice. This cocoon was to shroud me till I moved to a senior school in my early teens. I did once ask, when we were visiting a strongly loyalist part of Belfast, what the white-painted exhortations to 'Fuck the Pope' meant, but got no satisfactory answer; it did not even seem important enough to enquire who the pope was. His picture was not to be seen, whereas that of King Billy was everywhere, particularly as the Twelfth of July approached and ridiculous little men in tight blue suits and bowler hats began to march behind, to my mind, rather beautiful banners. I liked the sound of the thumping drums and piping flutes, and I loved the fat white horse and all the fringes and silver tassels. I was, however, furious when our journey to a picnic on the Antrim coast was impeded by the passage of one of the interminable Orange processions. It was in the village of Glynn, and I implored my mother to seize the opportunity of a slight gap in the marchers to nip over to the other side. The unanimous adult response was that this would be imprudent.

In mid-school years, some of my peer group, who were clearly well indoctrinated in matters of religious divides, would let drop a casual remark about someone's father owning a pawnshop or a chain of cheap clothing stores. Names beginning with Gold would provoke a furtive snigger. To belong to a family of fifteen seemed to me a privilege but I had no idea what it signified other than good fortune and possession of an income adequate to feed and clothe the brood.

To my shame I attempted to shake the faith of Annie, who continued to work for my mother and Aunt Rosemary after the deaths of Rosa and Stonard. Annie was a staunch Methodist whose personal discipline included rules which seemed to me silly, such as not eating bread that had been both buttered and jammed, not wearing any make-up, not using deodorants (in the belief that twice daily ablutions with Lifebuoy soap were sufficient – they were not!) and not marrying one's deceased sister's husband. She was to be confronted with the latter dilemma during the war, after the death of her own sister from tuberculosis (see 1941 diary). Annie never expressed dislike or suspicion of Roman Catholics, and I can see now that she possessed an unusually generous nature, fortified by unshakable faith. She put up smilingly with my interpretation of the origin of species and my insistence that the feeding mechanism of whales would have precluded one of them from having swallowed Jonah. Half a century later I apologised to her but she had quite forgotten my attempts to shake her beliefs.

The Derry relatives were, without any doubt, more stimulating than the Greenisland lot. Their vibrancy was often of a somewhat bizarre nature, and my interest in the unconventional, macabre or slightly sinister was aroused by hearing about some of my ancestors – the Stevenson equivalent of Auntie-Gertie-who-ran-away. There was 'Uncle Willie drowned in t'Foyle': someone, my father I suspect, made a sort of Stanley Holloway farce out of what must, after all, have been a family tragedy. I do not know when the event occurred but it appears he was on a bicycle and missed the way. Then it was revealed that Grandma's only sister, who appears in the family album wearing a crinoline, ringlets and lace pants, had been 'put away' in Letterkenny Asylum. Political correctness being unheard of then, such places were often referred to as the 'loony bin'. She had been a member of a party, led by Grandfather David, which went on a trip to Paris before the First World War, and there were vague whispers down the years about her incautious intake of French wines and unbridled behaviour, which had marred the holiday. Sadly, it seems, there may have been another alcoholic lurking in the woodwork.

Then there was Uncle John, who was held to be 'a little simple', but there is no indication of what form his simplicity took. He was not a sufferer from Down's syndrome; indeed, the sepia photograph shows a classically even-featured man with a goatee beard and benign expression. His hobbies were fox-terrier breeding and shooting in County Donegal, so presumably he was considered trustworthy with a gun. Poor thing, he was a frequent target for Madam's outbursts of vitriol and was known to have been reduced to tears at meal-times, the dining table being a favourite setting for scenes of family conflict. My mother, whose reticent nature was often affronted by the tirades of personal recrimination which ricocheted around the table, was always astonished at how quickly the air cleared for those directly engaged in battle - mostly Grandma and my father. The more sensitive onlookers were left feeling grazed, so to speak, by the flying glass.

One particularly poignant incident involved the unfortunate John, who had reached an age when nightly rising was a necessity. For some reason connected with hygiene and the breathing of 'pure air', Madam forbade the use of chamber pots, and it was a long, dark, cold linoleum walk from John's room to the bathroom. A greenish stain had been detected running down the roughcast wall just under John's bedroom window. With the opening of Madam's enquiry into the origins of the stain, 'All hell was let loose over the dinner table', and John was reduced to tears and admission of culpability. His last few years passed in peace and tranquillity, when my mother, who did not disallow chamber pots, moved in, and Madam moved out of the Collon House.

My father's half-brother Hugh had also been a target of Madam's unremitting criticism. In this case probably because of her extreme jealousy of Hugh's mother Maggie, who died in childbirth or not long after. No painting or photograph of Maggie survives, the only relics being a pair of mother-of-pearl opera glasses and a rat-tailed silver sauce spoon bearing her monogram. After an interval of mourning some considered indecently short, David remarried and Eileen assumed the role of wicked step-mother. Hugh's life between 1899 and 1917, when he was killed in action, was tragically inharmonious. During a childhood holiday at Drumaweir he confided in my mother that 'those diamond rings of hers can cut you know'.

3
GREENCASTLE

The Inishowen peninsula, separated from Northern Ireland by that arbitrary line drawn in 1921, lies in what was popularly called, at the time of which I am writing, the Free State. It never crossed my mind to enquire from what or whom it was free, but there did indeed seem to be a freedom of sun, sand, soft breezes, limitless waves, towering cliffs and whirling sea birds, which thrilled me as nothing before had done. Without doubt, then as now, it provided many getaway refuges and safe houses for terrorists, but one passed the border post at Muff with a nod and a smile and soon entered a different world, where trees became scarce and such as survived were bent to bonsai shapes by the relentless wind from the west. In adult life it is at Quigley's Point that I experience something akin to what a truffle-hunting pig must sense as it starts to dig. As a child I first felt the thrill on seeing Drumaweir Hotel at Greencastle, which was owned by friends of the family. It was a symmetrical mid-nineteenth-century house, not unlike that of the Greenisland grandparents, but the setting was less bleak and a wild garden ran down to the shore. Sheltered from the west wind, fuchsia, veronica, montbretia and rhododendrons flourished beside the little winding paths that led to a series of small sandy coves. In the evening one had to be very careful not to crush any of the numerous shiny black slugs that left their silvery trails everywhere. Silver traceries were also left by the small snails, whose striped shell colours ranged through yellow, orange, lilac, to brown and white. These could be found in even greater quantity among the marram grass in the dunes.

I remember Grandma scandalising the hotel guests by dancing up and down on the gravel outside the dining room window, dripping wet, hair all over the place, loudly proclaiming the delights of the dip she had just had, and urging others to do the same. 'Like a wild man from Borneo' was my mother's comment.

On the landing of the hotel was a very superior rocking-horse, the riding of which, without adult supervision, was forbidden. Children of more affluent parents were in the care of governesses but, as our finances did not stretch to such, I stood nowhere in the pecking order when it came to waiting for a turn; with few exceptions, they were a mean-spirited lot.

Picnic parties set out for the day from the hotel amid much loud discussion of where the wind would be least biting, who knew the most sheltered cove, who was to go in which car, how many buckets, spades and shrimping nets to take, and whether or not the adults would risk a swim. Picnic hampers were huge, and there was always a Primus stove to be struggled with by one or other of the uncles. All the children wore floppy cotton sunhats to protect them from sunstroke. There were multicoloured, segmented beach balls, which inevitably developed a leak before the day was out, tin-framed rackets, and sometimes a shuttlecock at which the adults made inefficient swipes, to peals of coy laughter from the auntie brigade. Children were supervised to the extent that one promised to go no further than a certain rock promontory, not to climb too high up or paddle further out than knee depth.

It was at one of these picnics that I became conscious of a fundamental difference between the sexes. Some children from the hotel were gathered in a shallow cave not far from the water's edge, when one of the boys chose to demonstrate his prowess at trajectory peeing: the arc glistened against the sunlight and his figure was silhouetted in the mouth of the cave. I was frustrated in not being able to see the source of the arc, and it was only after many years of determined searching in the *Encyclopaedia Britannica* for pictures of Greek and Roman statuary, Harmsworth's *Home Doctor* and *Anatomy for Artists*, that I finally got an approximate idea of what the male genitalia looked like. It seemed prudent not to relate the incident to my mother.

Among my mother's more shaming creations was an all-enveloping towelling changing tent with a drawstring around the neck. Under this one had to remove normal clothing and emerge bathing-suited, ready for the plunge. It was quite a feat to come out with arms and legs in the right holes and the shoulder buttons fastened. This prelude took any carefree element out of skipping down the beach to the sea. I also put on a gathered rubber mobcap, a blow-up ring, and sometimes even little soft rubber slippers, before finally getting wet.

Even in her own bedroom my mother undressed under a dressing-gown and would clutch it sharply together if anyone was so imprudent as to enter without knocking. I never saw her even partially naked until the indignity of extreme old age deprived her of choice.

Cowrie shells were to be found on some of the remoter strands of the Inishowen peninsula if one knew where to look, and it was enchanting to hear that they originated from the Indian Ocean. I loved the sculptured spaghetti-like casts the lugworms extruded on the otherwise smoothly rippled sand, like so many slubs in corded silk. It was tempting to squish them but I felt it would be some sort of sacrilege, even though I knew the next tide would wash them away.

It was not till many years later that I learned the joy of identifying different sea birds, so most were just 'gulls' at that time. Morbid interest was aroused if a pile of bones was discovered, and I used to make up stories about what had led to the demise. Mostly the remains were of some sheep which had lost its foothold or been scared over the edge: one time I was much distressed to find the remains of a collie dog, its long hair tangled among the bones. Prodding bundles of feathers at the foot of the cliffs always produced a cloud of winged activity and a curious smell, partly sea and weed but laced with a less attractive sweetish odour. Skates' eggs were satisfying to pop and thick-stalked branches of sea wrack gratifying to drag home, even though they so rapidly lost their glistening shine in a coating of sand. Blowholes tended to disappoint, as often the tide was not right and the hole not performing. When they did, it was ecstasy to stand among the tussocks of sea-pinks on the short clifftop grass, which was strewn with sharp twigs of brittle, barnacle-encrusted weed, waiting for the next deafening boom, accompanied by a shower of spray and flying spindrift. It added to the thrill to be told there was no land between me and North America.

It was at Fahan on Lough Swilly that I first visited a truly magnificent water garden. I must have been about four years old when my mother took me to visit a friend who had tamed a stream that flowed down from the twisted conifers at the top of her garden, through a series of little rock pools, in some of which were goldfish, to the shore below. There was a short waterfall between each pool and, *pièce de résistance*, a gnome with a fishing-rod, seated in his personal niche.

Stupendous sandcastles with battlements, moats and drawbridges were built to boost adult egos. Then there was the joy of burying all or much of oneself under wet sand, although this tended to be frowned upon. Indeed, the sand did persist in teeth, hair and clothing, got in the sandwiches, and infiltrated the car and finally one's bed.

Buckets of unfortunate anemones stuck to their rocks, shrimps, and sometimes a tiny fish or crab, were taken to the hotel room, on the strict understanding that they be returned to their pool the next morning.

We visited the rectory at Carndonagh, where the rector's wife, dressed elegantly in late-Edwardian style, presided. She wore a velvet neckband, to which was pinned a large cameo, and was said to be in delicate health. I was warned to keep an even lower profile than usual. Afternoon tea was served outside, rapidly cooling in fine, shallow, flower-sprigged cups with gold rims. I have a vague memory of sad comments being exchanged on my fatherless state, and some tut-tutting about the marital circumstances which had led to this. As almost always, I was the only child present.

In 1936 my mother decided to make her visits to the Free State less dependent on Grandma Stevenson's charity, so she bought a trailer and basic camping equipment. There were wooden tent-pegs, a mallet, stiff smelly groundsheets, canvas water-bags, aluminium and enamelled milk cans, lots of rope, and a tarpaulin to cover the lot. My aunt and her fiancé accompanied us on the first holiday, during which it rained so relentlessly that even my mother admitted defeat, and we spent some nights in an old army barracks, which dated from the days of the Black and Tans, near Dunaff Head.

The following year she went up-market and bought a secondhand caravan. We set off for the west of Ireland in a Morris 8, with a weak tow-bar which slowly bent near the middle, till the caravan rested on its front end and all the cupboards inside flew open. My mirth at the mess of sugar, tea and butter on the floor was not appreciated, any more than it was when Auntie Rosemary inadvertently whipped her own legs, rather than the offending dog, with the lead. The second night was spent in the yard of a garage repair shop in Athlone before we continued to Achill Island. There I began to see some point in this comfortless expedition. On Achill there was the lure of looking for amethysts, dodging the plague of violet-centred jellyfish, and going to the pier to choose from the abundance of fresh fish, lobsters and crabs.

Later we parked the caravan at Emlagh Point, near Roonagh Quay at Louisburg on Clew Bay, from where it was hoped to take a boat trip to Clare Island. Whether it was bad weather or unavailability of a willing boatman, I do not know, but we never got there. We stayed on land owned by heavy, black-clad Mrs McKail. My mother took a picture of her leaning, with wide, almost toothless grin, over the half-door of her traditional County Mayo cottage. She was insistently hospitable and took a genuine pleasure in letting us use her well (on the surface of which water-boatmen were always busy), eat her eggs and drink the warm milk fresh from her one cow. She tried to teach me how to milk, but I was revolted by the hot, sweet, steamy atmosphere and found the touch of the cow's udder repulsive. I imagine Mrs McKail had never encountered such a queasy child, and she was clearly disappointed that what she had thought of as a treat had misfired. She was a widow who had borne many children, all of whom were either dead or distant, but she seemed to accept her lot without self-pity and was grateful to have her cottage, the cow, a few hens, the neat turf-stack to keep the fire always alight, and an occasional visit from the parish priest. The more remote parts of Ireland are full of such strong, uncomplaining, resourceful women, whose lives have been touched by few of the so-called benefits of twentieth-century progress.

Writing of Mrs McKail reminds me of another woman who lived near Malin Head. She and her gentle-spoken, retired fisherman husband lived in a traditional Irish cottage: essentially a rectangle about twenty-four feet by twelve, the door in the middle, a small four-paned window each side of it, the open fire and cooking/sitting area on the left. A large bleached wooden dresser full of crockery faced the door: the bed was in a niche screened off by a rough hessian curtain. This woman spent most of her days in the company of her middle-aged, mentally defective daughter, making meals for her husband and any of the sons who happened to be working in the vicinity. The men scratched a living from poor, rock-strewn soil, going intermittently on fishing trips or to Scotland or England for seasonal work. Unashamed, she recounted how she had given birth to and raised twelve in the cottage. The damage to her daughter's brain took place at birth, when the child was delivered in a squatting position and its head struck the flagged stone floor. Some of her sons were 'good lads', others had married girls with notions above their station and moved to Lifford. Two were engaged in activities of which she clearly disapproved. In 1972 she wrote me a three-page letter which could just as well be written today:

> I be at my Husband Patrick Joseph to write to yurs but he is a bad writer or speller so he says to write yourself. I am not much good at the pen, so it is a shame to not write more oftener days goes to weeks and weeks to months, but anyhow we hope that these trouble makers will soon settle down and stop there cruel carry on. I say if they had to work harder for a living like other people fighting and shooting would be more trouble to them but suppose they are all payed to well to settle down. Well I read in a Newspaper the other day where a fellow put a bomb in his car and made of to Lifford to a dance Hall to blow it

up but before he got out of his car the damed thing blew up and pieces of him was never seen wasent he entightled to the benefit of it himself instead of Hundreds of innocent people killed.

4
Knock and Gilnahirk

Some time after we moved to Knock I became vaguely aware that to have two parents was the norm. In order to satisfy anyone curious enough to ask, I was told to explain that my father was abroad in India, or was it Africa? I hated it when people did ask, as early geography lessons, when much time was spent colouring red those parts of the world that constituted the British Empire, had added to my confusion. Both countries were pendulous, one smaller than the other and more pointed. I remained unclear as to where my father was to be found. He was, in fact, in Worthing, living, between incarcerations for his alcoholism, with a woman who ran kennels and was better able than my mother to tolerate his behaviour.

Absence of a father did not at that time worry me nearly as much as not having any companions of my own age. Fraternisation with neighbouring children, of whom there were few, was discouraged. I suspect my mother felt that closer acquaintance might evoke greater familiarity with the parents, and consequent unwelcome enquiry into her marital status. She was always to remain an intensely private person, who went to some pains to emphasise that she enjoyed her own company.

We lived on the outer fringes of Belfast, where the midsummer grate of the corncrake was taken for granted, scythes rather than combine harvesters were still used, and neat conical haystacks with little stone-weighted rope caps were part of the summer scene. These were tempting to play around, but the dust always brought on attacks of asthma and hay fever, not to mention adult disapproval.

The public elementary school was about a mile 'up the hill' just outside Gilnahirk village on the lower Braniel. The building dated from the early nineteenth century, a long, white, one-storey roughcast building set on the banks of the upper reaches of the Connswater river. The lavatories were in a row outside. Although free, the school was not deemed suitable for me. Nits and other forms of contamination, such as the acquisition of a local accent, precluded my attendance. It was also, of course, coeducational, and as my mother invariably dubbed all boys nasty, dirty, rough and noisy, the prospect of my mixing with them was not even considered. I never got nits, nor did I become able with any certainty to identify a nit-infested head, although I always closely inspected those in front of me in the local bus. Fleas were a more serious threat: they were common in public transport and cinemas in those days, and they just loved me. My reaction was severe, and I itch even now at the recall of those hard, red, excruciatingly itchy weals that lasted for days, ending up watery and crusty, stuck to my black woollen school stockings.

My mother had few friends, and such as she had lived at a considerable distance; a crosstown trip was necessary in order to have afternoon tea and that I might 'play' with some sanitised boy or girl. More often than not there was no other child to enliven the afternoon, and if the hosts happened not even to possess a domestic pet, the hours would drag interminably. Some kindly 'uncle' would try to entertain me but it was heavy going for everyone.

Very soon after we moved to Knock my mother advertised for a reliable person to take care of me on week-day afternoons. Our first encounter I do not remember, but Mrs Nancy Anderson, hereafter referred to as San, came into my life and provided something elusive that I had never previously experienced in a grown-up person. Undoubtedly she was an authority figure but she was never sharp or admonitory and she laughed a lot. Her job was to take me for healthy walks and prepare supper on our return. At first a pushchair was brought along in case I should tire, but this was soon dispensed with. Our progress was slow because of the many stops we made to pass the time of day with villagers, who would suddenly appear over the hedge just as we were passing, and protracted chats with the Cherryvalley shopkeepers. This introduced me to a sociable side of life I had not known before. All my mother's sorties were in the car. I do not remember ever walking into the village, or indeed anywhere else with her: so neighbourhood contacts were strictly limited and I do not believe she ever became wholly reconciled to her reduced situation.

When San and I went to the village there would be small shopping commissions, and I enjoyed each shop for its particular atmosphere. Harvard's, the main grocer, stood on its own, a cut above the rest of the shops, which had been purpose-built in a row of identical design. Mr Harvard and his wife lived over the shop, adjacent to which were his garage, petrol pump and bicycle repair shop. The main attraction at Harvard's was the bacon slicer, beside which could be found delicious morsels of raw bacon to chew. I had to be sneaky about this after an initial lecture on the subject of hygiene and the disease-carrying nature of flies. All too often Mr Harvard had a bandage on one of his remaining fingers: the rest were pinkish-purple, shiny stumps. Later I was to be told about the life-cycle of the tapeworm. We met a farmer's wife from Portaferry who related how a thirty-three foot worm had been removed from her husband's bowel: this news item finally killed my appetite for raw bacon. Harvard's always smelled slightly of paraffin, and my mother claimed that the vegetables sometimes tasted of it – not surprising, as they lay in open boxes not far from the firelighters. Mother rarely patronised the shop, as she disapproved of the sticky flypapers which hung, thickly encrusted with corpses and still living flies, desperately trying to free themselves. As she herself kept wasp and slug-traps, I did not follow the logic, though I agreed with her about the flies.

The line of shops began with Miss Irvine's, the confectioner, tobacconist and newsagent. San and Miss Irvine were on familiar terms and often discussed the shortcomings of the other shops in the row, the butcher and fishmonger at the other end arousing most criticism on the grounds of dirty premises and inflated prices. In between were the hairdresser, the post office, the chemist and a haberdasher, into whose shop we seldom went, as my mother pronounced their stock lamentably deficient.

San lived at that time in Ballyhackamore just off the Upper Newtownards Road, so it was a tribute to her genuine interest in people, and her pleasant personality, that she so quickly became part of the Cherryvalley scene. Some years later she moved house to the Gilnahirk Road. The one shop we never patronised was that of the hairdresser: my hair got squarely cut at home, the neck clipped with tickly shears, and a miserably wispy fringe was created to hide my 'too-high' forehead. What with that, sticking-out ear, freckles and buck teeth, I was not a particularly comely child.

San, however, did patronise the hairdresser, who tortured her hair until there was scarcely any left. The permanent wave of the time was ruinous to all but the toughest hair, so frequent perms, combined with bleach, left her hair in a sorry condition. Frizz followed frizz, but she was always hopeful that the next time it would be better. When the perm was failing she resorted to curling tongs and metal curlers. In old age she accumulated an assortment of wigs provided by the NHS, which she invariably ruined with misguided washing techniques. Hats in the early 1930s still retained something of the cloche shape of the 1920s, and San pinned quite convincing false curls under the brim at each side. Her huge blue eyes, classic bone structure and lovely skin that tanned in summer, made up for the disastrous hair.

My mother had beautiful auburn hair with a slight wave, but the fashion of the day dictated that this too should be tortured into a crop of small sausage rolls at the front and a Claudette Colbert fringe. Denied the Shirley Temple look, I agitated for pigtails but was told that my hair was too fine and meagre for that too. Years later, after a succession of permanent waves not much more succe than San's (see 1948 diary), I discovered that my hair was quite abundant and a not altogether unattractive colour.

Mr Shillington, the chemist, was rotund, with pink and white skin and snowy hair. Steely grey eyes darted suspiciously behind steel-rimmed spectacles, and he did not encourage small talk, so transactions were strictly formal. Jessie, his daughter, was also pink and plump but more forthcoming, and took charge of the cosmetic section. By the mid-1930s a modicum of make-up no longer stamped one as of dubious virtue, but restraint had still to be used. Nails could be polished with a chamois buffer, or possibly even given a coat of very pale pink varnish. No 'lady', however, ever varnished her toenails. Eye make-up was practically non-existent, apart from crude boxes of mascara for the very 'fast', but there was a large choice of lipsticks, and rouge was permitted as it was supposed to impart a healthy glow. San was not too hot on the rouging and often got one cheek slightly higher than the other, but her lovely bone structure overcame any possible clownish effect.

The butcher and his brother were a humourless pair who weighed down to the last ounce, watching the scales keenly till there was not the slightest tremor. Strangely enough, I did not then associate meat and the butchery trade with animal suffering, there being no TV to bring the gruesomely bloody reality of the slaughterhouse into the living room. I do not remember many details about our meals, except that they were entirely adequate. Not nearly so much emphasis was put on food and balanced diet in those days and, possibly in consequence, there was general preoccupation with the threat of constipation. One was well advised to claim having 'gone', otherwise a block-buster Bile Bean, or worse, the rubber 'squeezer' might be resorted to. My mother always provided lots of vegetables, so thankfully I did not often have to lie, but having submitted a couple of times to the indignity and discomfort of the enema, I always claimed to have 'been'.

Even during the war our diet remained healthy. The 'herrin'-alive' man still came every Friday with his cart, yelling loudly that they were fresh from Ardglass and cost one penny each. A buttermilk cart also toured our neighbourhood, and most people grew some vegetables. Mr Ewing was the proprietor of our fish shop, where more exotic varieties than were available from the cart were obtainable. With no great subtlety, he was generally known as Fishface Ewing. His face was long, lugubrious and greyish-white, with almost colourless eyes, no eyelashes to speak of, and a round hole of a mouth that never quite closed. He was not above passing off a greening fillet on me and could even speak of it in laudatory tones: 'That's a greeat bit a fish; yer Mommy'll jest luv it.' Once there was a complaint, after which I was embarrassed to enter the shop.

Sweets were not too great a problem. I think the threat of over-indulgence was more in my mother's mind than in fact. I liked the occasional one and was particularly attracted to huge multicoloured gobstoppers, which I saw other children buying, but from which I was always dissuaded. It would have been so easy just to give me one to assuage my curiosity, but instead they came to represent some sort of forbidden fruit, until eventually I plucked up courage defiantly to spend my Saturday penny on some. A small paper bag contained very few of those revolting marble-sized sweets. I was very disappointed and puzzled as to the vagaries of human taste. Sherbet barrels were attractive too, but had also to be concealed as they were deemed a working-class taste. These minor acts of defiance came, of course, later on, when I had a modicum of freedom to cycle to and from school and visit the houses of approved friends. San's duties by that time amounted to little more than occasional help at home, as my mother by then shared the services of Annie, who lived with Auntie Rosemary in the house next to ours.

Sometimes San could be persuaded to go as far as the main Upper Newtownards Road or out to the gates of the parliament building at Stormont. En route we would make a visit to another post office run by a Valkyrie-type woman who wore her hair in massive blond plaits curled around each ear; not until I saw *Star Wars* did I see their equal. Outside her office we waited to see the Prince of Wales (later Edward VIII), with whom I was at the time infatuated, come to open parliament. Royalty was not as fine a spectacle as I had hoped, although I liked the hat with what looked like a bunch of bananas on top, and waved my Union Jack dutifully. My mother could just remember being taken to see Queen Victoria and being likewise somewhat disappointed at seeing a small, black, hunched-up figure in an open carriage. Mother was a great flag woman: she was obsessed with it being the right way up, and I was early taught about the multiple components of the Union Jack and how to draw it accurately. We even flew one from the attic window for the Coronation in 1937.

Any milk of human kindness to be found in our house was of the distinctly skimmed variety. Strict observance of the superficial social niceties was insisted upon, and it was assumed that one was at all times truthful and, outwardly at least, deferential to the wisdom of one's elders. I do not remember hearing generous praise or admiration voiced about any of our acquaintances, nor do I remember my mother expressing an intent to visit anyone without the prefix: 'I really ought to go and see. . .' The critical faculty was finely developed but charity, forgiveness and generosity of spirit were attitudes that never came under discussion. The word 'love' was almost pathologically avoided, and pragmatism ruled. Greetings consisted of perfunctory pecks on the cheek or a hand formally shaken, the clasp to be firm and on no account clammy or sweaty. Emotions were to be kept strictly under control and teeth gritted in the face of pain. My mother claimed not to have cried out in childbirth, her only experience of which took place when she was in her thirties, at home and without anaesthetic. When my own time came to deliver, I had a distinct feeling of having let the side down by bawling loudly. My mother also claimed to have watched with interest the stitching of a wound in her hand. Surely there was some link in her attitude towards pain and forbearance and her disdain of men who had not offered their lives for disposal in the name of patriotism. I remember talk of white feathers and conscientious objectors, but I was too young to grasp what it was all about. In my teens, when I was flaunting my agnosticism, left-wing political and republican sympathies, as well as my commitment to the free-love ideal, I caused additional pain by expressing admiration for those men who had the courage of their conviction that it was evil to kill no matter how seemingly good the cause. I never actually *met* one of these men till many years later, and a dreary wimp he was.

Early in the war the subject of venereal disease became, even to my mother, unavoidable, as there was a press campaign urging us neither to contract nor to spread it. My persistent questions as to the nature of what it was we were not to spread and how, really embarrassed my mother, whose own knowledge of sexually transmitted diseases was practically nil. If one takes into account that when my mother was about to be married, Rosa's only pre-nuptial comment was that there were some aspects of married life that women just had to put up with and that she supposed my mother knew about them anyhow, it is not surprising she found it difficult to discuss any sex-related topic.

We always had dogs, and dogs tend to be uninhibited in their display of sharp, bright pink penises; donkeys drag it on the ground, and even sparrows mount each other, so I continued to press the questions with relentless regularity at each birthday: 'Well, is it like dogs and can you do it only at certain times like being on heat?' That one really put her on the spot and she admitted that one could 'do it' more or less at any time. The argument that I was not yet old enough did not subdue me, and my retort was always that if I was old enough to ask I was old enough to understand any forthcoming explanation. Harmsworth's *Home Doctor* was not as enlightening as I hoped, but persevering study of it left me convinced that I had piles, tuberculosis and venereal diseases of several sorts, and that I was possibly heading towards general paralysis of the insane, with a face like Baudelaire or the noseless man who sold newspapers opposite the City Hall in Belfast.

San had the gift of saying quite outrageous things about people, their behaviour or appearance, but without malice or rancour. Throughout her life, friends and relatives 'put upon' her, and she would complain at length but without bitterness, laughing at the same time about their idiosyncrasies. Her sister Molly Millar lived in Carrickfergus, which made visits to Knock something of an undertaking and therefore, to San's relief, infrequent.

Molly was older than San and she looked like a giant pouter pigeon, plump, with a heaving breast and tiny feet. Rather than cooing, however, Molly rasped, in the way unique to women raised in or near Dublin. Her nose was Roman and she always wore a heavy hat, which she was reluctant to remove even in the house. I suppose she felt it strengthened her authority. Molly had married 'up', whereas San had married either slightly 'down' or sideways. I think, in retrospect, that this was an ongoing source of irritation to Molly, whose tone of voice nearly always conveyed reproach or criticism, as she fired relentless questions, often loaded with innuendo, at whoever was in range. Even as a small child I was not spared: she was naturally curious about my mother's marital situation, and I felt that while

I was regarded with some degree of pity, there was neither warmth nor compassion.

San suffered interminable advice from Molly on how better to order her house, husband, garden, wardrobe and, when finances got strained, the lodgers. San had another blight visited upon her for a while in the presence of her husband's senile mother, a sweet-looking, fragile old lady, dressed invariably in Edwardian black. She had finally to be sent to a home after developing the habit of lurking behind doors, bread-knife in hand. I do not think Molly really expected her advice to be acted upon, and inaction gave her the excuse to renew the assault at a later date. Her own husband was understandably a man economic with words: he had a high glistening dome of a head, from which protruded a lump of considerable size on which nobody ever commented. It was one of those things which both fascinate and repel, and I suspect it ultimately had something to do with his death. Any joy these two may have experienced went out of their lives when news came that their only child, Jimmy, a pilot in the RAF, had disappeared without trace over mountainous terrain in Sicily (see 1941 diary). Poor Molly never really recovered from the shock and there were shaming incidents of mid-life shoplifting which were attributed to her lasting sense of loss.

Molly's husband got on well with Mr San, who tended to come home late on the days of Molly's visits. The men would escape to the garden to discuss boats, cars, dogs and ferrets. I fear the ferret was not well kept. There was a cage hung at adult chest height from the garage wall, and inside an angry, churning, snapping creature with wicked little amber eyes. The smell was overpowering as there was always a faecal trickle running down the wall from the cage. What, if anything, Mr San ever caught or hoped to catch with it I was not told. He was a kind man, somewhat slow in manner and intellect, and I think he very much regretted the childlessness of his marriage. He owned a garage in York Street and, in the days before the business failed, always had a car of his own. From what I overheard, his trusting nature allowed too many customers to build up credit, often falling for the line that they would settle for sure the next week.

Before the war, when petrol rationing put an end to almost all pleasure trips, I would occasionally be allowed to accompany Mr and Mrs San for a whole day's outing. Sometimes we would go out in the pony-trap he had bought, or travel by car to Strangford Lough, where he had a small boat moored, and fish for mackerel. I hated the bit when he had to bonk them on the head, but I forgave him as he was not by nature cruel. My mother refused to eat the fish, saying, with some truth, that anything coming out of Strangford Lough near the Comber estuary was bound to have been scavenging on sewage. If we went further down the Ards peninsula, lobsters could be bought at Portavogie or Ardglass, blue and with their poor claws tied with string. They would miserably scrabble, first around the boot of the car, and ultimately around the bottom of our gas-heated clothes boiler. I remained unconvinced that they were 'just going peacefully to sleep' and suspect my mother felt the same, but the operation, once begun, had to reach its logical conclusion.

Why fizzy drinks were disallowed at home is not clear, as this was before the deleterious effect on teeth of all things sweet became so widely recognised, but at San's there was always a steady supply of lemonade. Another delicacy to be enjoyed there was butter-beans, a simple enough taste, but as I was unable adequately to describe them they never appeared at home. San kept a continuous supply of stewed tea on the stove and at the table, which was permanently laid for a meal. It made no great difference whether it was to be the midday or evening meal, there was always lots of Big White Chief loaf, jam, sugar and butter, and a bottle of HP sauce.

San claimed to have had at least half her stomach removed, and to subsist on a diet strictly limited by medical prohibitions. Whatever the advice, it can surely not have recommended bread, jam, and almost everything fried, from the eggs and bacon to bits of soda bread, potato bread and sausages. Vegetables, if they appeared on her menu at all, were long boiled and mostly of the root variety. Salads were rare on San's table, although lettuce, tomatoes and radishes were grown in her garden, alongside the sweetpeas she loved so much.

I cannot remember any alcohol being drunk in the house, but there were times when it was clear that Mr San was in disgrace and that this had something to do with the hour at which, and the state in which, he had returned from his garage in York Street the previous night.

San smoked anything from Player's Navy Cut to Craven A, and kept a dangling catkin of ash trembling over everything, from the table as she laid it to the washing-up bowl, often humming tunelessly or muttering her thoughts through the smokescreen.

The nearest source of cigarettes was at Ann Quinn's shop at the bottom of the Gilnahirk Road, to which San often sent me for a fresh supply. My dread was very real at the thought of the reception I would invariably get from Ann, who ran a general store from the ground floor of her solid, pebble-dashed house, which stood squarely by itself, set back from the road, with no fence, hedge or tree to soften the bleak frontage. Anyone unwise enough to prop a bicycle against the shop window provoked a blast of abuse from within, to be followed by a more specific complaint on entering the shop. The forecourt was bare of bench or object of any kind, so bicycles had to be left recumbent while the owner negotiated with Ann. Suspense was sometimes heightened by a long wait before she emerged from the back regions which could just be glimpsed from the counter. The shop did not smell fresh: an odour of decaying vegetables, paraffin oil and general dustiness hung overall, and the sweets were often stale, reluctant to release their sticky hold on the sides of the large glass jars.

Ann's hair, or it may have been a wig, was kept in order by a hair-net, the elastic of which cut into her forehead; wig or hair, the texture was of dusty felt. Ann could well have been the prototype for Grandma in the Giles cartoons. I never saw her wearing anything other than a sleeveless overall in dark-blue cotton with a pattern of small flowers. Ribbed woollen sleeves protruded from the armholes, and thick lisle stockings wrinkled down into fur-rimmed tartan slippers. Incurably crabbed, her invariable greeting was a rasping, 'Well, whatdyerwant?' Certainly, where children were concerned, every transaction was tinged with suspicion. Aware of the risk of provoking an outburst, one trod carefully and exuded sycophantic respect, but sooner or later something would set her off. Producing a note or coin which demanded too much change was bound to invoke muttering, and often disappearance into the back regions. Momentarily to forget what it was one had been sent for, or to be a bit slow getting money out of the purse, was also a fault. To refer to a note was probably worst of all, especially if it had to be handed over; she had difficulty in reading and did not want this fact exposed.

San, however, was a favoured customer, as she also came originally from the Free State, although San's origins were in Swords, near Dublin, and Ann's were in County Clare. There was some sort of bond, however, and San was sometimes invited into the back kitchen to take a cup of the strong tea that simmered on the range. Ann had a 'niece' who lived on the premises and went out to work, although she sometimes helped in the shop. Possibly she *was* a niece, as one could not imagine Ann ever having been 'taken advantage of'.

Poor Ann got beaten up by a pioneer group of urban thugs who got away with a very small sum of money from the till. The shock, however, was so great that Ann sold up and returned to her native county in the west of Ireland.

I would sometimes be sent to Flynn's Nursery in Cherryvalley to buy lettuce, tomatoes or, occasionally, soft fruits. 'Fat' Flynn and his father ran the nursery on a large site in Cherryvalley in the days when it warranted that name, and half a century before it disappeared under a wealth of ugly red-brick executive-style houses.

Neither Fat nor his father was really fat, just what is termed in Ulster 'well built'. How they made a living out of the nursery is a mystery, as there was evidence everywhere of incompetence, neglect and stultifying lethargy. Despite the fact that our own garden was large, we never grew tomatoes, and a glut of lettuce would be followed by a gap before the next lot matured. I quite often made the long trudge up a stony, weed-infested tract to the main glasshouse, which also served as the office – a fact made known by a torn-off piece of cardboard, pierced with a bit of string, which hung crookedly on the invariably open door. Much of the glass was cracked and some panes were missing – and there was seldom any sign of either Fat or his father. A search then ensued, often down at the stream that runs at the bottom of the valley, a clear-running tributary of what turns into the muddy Connswater river and finally emerges in an insalubrious part of Belfast Lough near the harbour airport. Fat, or more often his father, finally run to ground, would then lumber up to the office and discuss what they had, or more often had not, got for sale. Flower pots were stacked in corners, miniature towers of Pisa, cracked, exuding sandy soil and withered skeletons of what had once been chrysanthemums or azaleas. Fat's father was benign and patient while one fumbled for the money, which he would put in his battered tin box along with bits of grubby twine and faded plant labels. Nothing seemed to have been watered for a long time, although there was a permanently dripping tap and a length of hose just outside.

Old Mrs Flynn was known to be alive but was never sighted. Gossip had it that Fat had a relationship with a sad-looking emaciated woman with peroxide hair and broken front teeth, which she tried to disguise with white sticking plaster. It was said that her husband knew all about Fat, but the teeth indicated that he may not have been a wholly compliant cuckold.

Fat had a fine tenor voice and modelled himself on Count John McCormack and Caruso. He was much in demand to perform at village hall concerts. In the early days of the war regular entertainments still took place in the heavily blacked-out, dimly blue-lit hall, and I used to sit riveted in expectation, clutching my gas-mask in its box on my knee.

Fat's appearance on stage never varied: small moustache, black Brylcreemed hair, a slightly too tight suit in quite a large black and white hound's-tooth check, yellow tie and 'co-respondent' (two-tone) shoes. His repertoire was not extensive: 'Trees', 'I Hear You Calling Me', 'Pale Hands I Loved beside the Shalimar', 'Come into the Garden, Maud', 'I'll Walk beside You' and 'The Rose of Tralee'. He was hugely popular and would come graciously back for encore after encore. Fat would be followed by a troupe of overweight tap-dancers, upholstered in petunia satin, and a child prodigy who did imitations of Shirley Temple. He had a female counterpart in terms of competence and bulk, if not quite in popularity. She was a massive blancmange of middle-aged coyness whose favourite songs were 'The

Merry, Merry Pipes of Pan', 'Cherry Ripe' and wartime favourites such as 'The White Cliffs of Dover' and 'A Nightingale Sang in Berkeley Square'. Afterwards we would stumble our way out and walk home to equally blacked-out houses, hoping the air-raid sirens would not go again that night.

Fat drove an ambulance and helped at the first-aid and bandaging classes that were held in the primary school up the Braniel. My mother and San dutifully attended and studied their St John's Ambulance books, practising on each other and on me. San was not gifted but eventually passed her certificate of competence; thankfully neither of them ever had to put their skills into practice.

My mother must have been deeply disappointed by my craven comportment when introduced to the joys of horsewomanship. By the time I was first put on a pony, her financial situation was precarious and, her own horses having been sold, she was reduced to riding other people's when they were in need of exercise – or so it was claimed. In reality, I think her friends must have sensed that means were very slender and taken pity on her. We went regularly to an indoor school in Comber, where what was claimed to be a docile mount would be produced for me. The only thing I really enjoyed was feeding the horses sugar lumps and carrots, and stroking their responsive ears and velvety muzzles. I liked watching the grooms brushing the horses and tried hard to emulate the 'ssss'-ing sound they made between their teeth as they wielded the brush. Once I was on board, the horse invariably sensed that a timid, under-sized novice was in the saddle and behaved accordingly. It was not entirely owing to ineptitude that my first lesson in cantering ended with me dangling by one stirrup, bumping along the thankfully fairly soft ground surface of the indoor school for a seemingly interminable time before the horse was brought to a standstill amid adult exclamations about the girths not having been tight enough.

Attached by a leading rein to my mother's horse, I would walk and trot around the undulating drumlin country of North Down, until eventually I was allowed to go solo, it being thought that by that time I had some control. The ponies drank long and to their total satisfaction at any opportunity, and there was one particularly humiliating incident when I slid off a Shetland pony's narrow shoulders on to the rough, wet gravel beside the watering-trough on the Gilnahirk Road. My mother rode ahead, urging me to remount and assert my authority, taking little notice of my wails till she saw that I was indeed spitting blood and that a few teeth, which had in any case been loose, were missing. The watering-trough was not far from the council house where the numerous O'Shaughnessy family lived. They came under discussion from time to time by the adults, in terms of wonder, abhorrence, disdain or, occasionally, sympathy for Mrs O'Shaughnessy's dreary lot in life. At what, if anything other than making more children, her husband worked is not on record; he remains in memory a faint figure moving slowly around the garden between their back door and the outside lavatory. There were seventeen children of strikingly similar appearance, coming down the scale like a Russian wooden-doll set, till the last was very small indeed. All had straight fair hair, pasty faces, and noses so tilted that one could see up the nostrils; all had squints and wore round steel-rimmed spectacles, and several of them came to gloat over my discomfiture. Mrs O'Shaughnessy was not on San's chat list, so the ultimate fate of the family goes unrecorded, although I remember it being remarked, somewhat patronisingly, that some of the older children had got employment and seemed to be doing quite well. All had been processed at the Braniel school till they reached the leaving age of fourteen.

Penurious though we were, and unpromising horsewoman that I was, money was found to turn me out like a Thelwell cartoon child. We went to Mr Grimshaw in Glengall Street, where a fine hound's-tooth tweed was selected for the jacket and I was measured for jodhpurs. My mother, in her great innocence about sexual matters, failed to notice how long Mr Grimshaw lingered on the inside-leg measurement, often re-checking it. When I reminisced on the subject many years later, her response was: 'Oh, surely not, you must have imagined it.' It was the same with her old schoolfriend's husband, who volunteered to give me driving lessons when I was seventeen. She did not want to know and found it embarrassing that I was unwilling to continue with the lessons. As well as the natty little jacket, I had a black velvet hat and a miniature ivory-handled crop with which to chastise my pony. By the beginning of the war petrol rationing precluded further trips to Comber; many of the horses were pensioned off, or worse, and the riding came to a natural end.

About the same time as the riding lessons, there were

weekly remedial exercise sessions at Miss Foster's School of Dance on the Lisburn Road. I did not have knock knees any more, nor did I bite my nails, which were at one time dipped in bitter aloes to break the habit, which was viewed with almost the same horror as masturbation would have been. The latter was a practice I did not hear about till years later, and I doubt if my mother even knew about such a possibility, otherwise she would have thought up a deterrent. My sticking-out left ear caused such concern that it was taped to my head with plaster each night before I went to bed.

Dancing lessons were another form of purgatory. My first teacher, Miss Leila Corry, was considered 'fast', as she wore a thick coating of carmine lipstick and matching long nails, like the witch in Disney's *Snow White.* For classes she wore tights and an exiguous pleated skirt. Her teaching style would have delighted Joyce Grenfell. The house on the Upper Newtownards Road where the lessons took place was large, and it was approached by a long, tree-lined avenue. No Mr Corry was ever encountered, but it is hard to believe that the house and its considerable grounds were kept going on fees from the School of Dance alone. Leila would have been an admirer of Isadora Duncan, the Denises and Martha Graham, and she must have found her pupils an unimaginative, leaden-footed lot. I remember being acutely embarrassed at being asked to mime the planting of bulbs in the parquet floor, the chasing of butterflies with a net, and other sylvan frolics. She would not accept that some young spines are not double-jointed and that to kneel and bend over backwards till one's head touched the floor was for some an impossibility. Faced with protest, she tried a bit of force. I recall the excruciating pain, and to this day doctors ask me if I suffered early injury.

Happily, lessons with Miss Corry did not last long before I was inscribed to join Miss Lena King's Ballet School. At this type of dance too I proved a disappointment. None of the class had ever seen a live performance, so the only model of what we were aiming at was our well-upholstered teacher, who was reputed once to have been a member of the *corps de ballet* at Sadlers Wells. The misery of my ineptitude was heightened by the fact that my mother was the only parent who sometimes sat and watched during practice sessions. There was always a post-mortem on the way home as to my apparent inability to keep time to the music, and the lack of delicacy in my hand and arm movements. Notwithstanding this lack of talent I appeared in Miss King's annual display on the stage of the now sadly demolished Empire Theatre, as a clumping member of a Tally-Ho quartet, a cygnet from a simplified version of the quartet in *Swan Lake*, and in a Grecian barefoot hoop dance where I distinguished myself by forgetting to take off my shoes till the curtain was rising. The outbreak of war thankfully signalled the end of attempts to teach me either to ride or to dance.

My experience of live theatre went little further than an annual visit to Jimmy O'Dea's pantomime, which also took place at the Empire Theatre. This building would now undoubtedly qualify to be listed – it was slightly reminiscent of the Moulin Rouge, its angles picked out by multicoloured electric bulbs. I was taken to see Jean Forbes-Robertson, flying around on unfortunately very perceptible wires, as Peter Pan at the Royal Opera House. Ballet companies first began to visit Belfast shortly after the war, so only then was I finally able to appreciate this art form, which encompasses virtually all the sculptural, musical, lyrical and visual arts, the most basic skills towards which Miss King's largely ungifted pupils had long been striving. Some of the young dancers of that time later became famous, and are now sadly dead. John Gilpin and Eric Bruhn were clearly heading for greater heights, and I was fortunate enough to attend many performances by the then slender Kenneth MacMillan and by Celia Franca, who later formed her own company in Canada.

My mother's interests were extraordinarily diverse. At one time she went to tap-dancing classes with Auntie Rosemary. At roughly the same time she was attending lectures on astronomy at the Royal Observatory in Armagh. Her taste in literature ranged from the lurid historical novels of Philip Lindsay, to reading all the works of Robert Graves and Anthony Trollope. She was also curiously attached to *Lettres de Mon Moulin* by Alphonse Daudet, and *Heloise and Abelard* as depicted by her contemporary at school, Helen Waddell. I think she felt some reflected glory in the acquaintance. She often referred to another school friend, one Chattie MacIldooey, who had 'bolted' from the stifling cultural backwater of Northern Ireland to the fast life in London, where she married into theatrical circles and became the mother of Angela Lansbury.

There was almost always some ambitious project on my mother's workshop bench: quite complicated things, like a doll's house for the dolls I was supposed not to enjoy playing with, a big box for the doomed tortoises to hibernate in, toy boats which never proved stable when launched, and – later in life – ghastly 1950s 'contemporary' coffee tables with splayed legs. She made miniature rock gardens from small stones, using sealing-wax for the flowers and tiny bits of mirror where water was represented: these were set in iridescent bowls and sold to Magee's art shop in Belfast.

During the war she resorted to dressmaking to eke out our income. Of this activity I was deeply ashamed. For the same snobbish reasons I felt regret that the family business had been a bakery rather than what I then deemed a more respectable line, such as shipbuilding, linen goods or munitions manufacture. Awareness of the subtle divide between the trades and professions did not hit me till my teens, when such trivia were much discussed at school.

My mother's training of other people's horses to jump bizarre objects was another activity about which I had mixed feelings, especially when a photograph of her seated on a dappled steed, in a jump over a wheelbarrow, appeared in the *Belfast Telegraph.* My friends regarded this feat with a mixture of admiration and ridicule. I much preferred the long-gone image of my mother on a side-saddle, wearing full riding-habit, taken at the Dublin Horse Show of 1926.

Then there was her garden, of which I remember every detail, as much of my time was spent cutting the four separate lawns – three pence was the going rate per lawn. (See 1941 diary for slavery in garden.) The plot on which our house stood was an uninspiring long narrow rectangle, so in an attempt to break the monotony, it had been divided into four entirely different sections, a lawn in the middle of each. Gravel access paths ran up each side and traversed the middle, and a high privet hedge screened us from neighbours. Crannies for weeds were everywhere, as every flowerbed was edged with sharp Scrabo stone (Scrabo being a hill in County Down) and there was quite an area of rockery to weed as well as the gravel paths that had to be raked. My mother liked the speed with which *lonicera* grew, and embarked on several exercises in topiary: her most successful were a cat and a peacock that grew on either side of the path to the front door. Behind the house were two parallel rockeries divided by yet another gravel path and stone steps which led to the pond lawn. Here edges reached ludicrous levels: the pond was round, but set in a square of crazy-paving, at each corner of which was a small flowerbed eighteen inches square. I am sure my mother got her greatest satisfaction from designing the garden, rather than from its maintenance or products. She had singlehandedly dug the hole for the pond, lined it with a wooden mould and poured the cement, at about the same time as she first explored the delights of camping and caravanning.

The third lawn had four apple trees and a large vegetable bed along one side. A peculiar mixture was grown here, of which I remember a glut of leeks, which were Mr Boyd's speciality, purple sprouting broccoli, redcurrants and raspberries. In the choice of what was to be grown I think my mother had to submit to the whims of Mr Boyd, who came once a week only. The top part of the garden, most distant from the house, was divided off by an Australian laurel hedge and was devoted to the manure pit and the pets' cemetery.

Mr Boyd, who was pinkly bald and always wore a shirt with a stud but no collar, was not inclined to conversation, but he was kind enough and tolerated my hovering presence. He even once tried to teach me how to use a scythe, but his methods of dealing with slugs and snails I found disgusting. He kept a jam pot of strong saline solution into which they were mercilessly dropped and which he seldom emptied, so the resulting brew was a thick, creamy froth. I once found a massive column of snails wrapped around one of the pergolas, well hidden in the depths of the lovely pink rambler roses my mother later expunged because she did not like pink. Although I kept quiet about my discovery, inevitably Mr Boyd found the colony and duly despatched the lot. He would show me where the blackbird's nest was (see 1941 diary), but his patience was sorely tried by our tortoises, which, although tethered by a fine string led through a hole drilled in their shells, were expert hedge climbers and were repeatedly getting wedged in situations from which they had laboriously to be untwined and removed.

Mr Boyd and my mother respected each other, although they had differences of opinion on how many leek beds to plant, how and when to prune the redcurrants, and the treatment of blight on the apple trees. Mr Boyd, who had won prizes for his enormous leeks, nearly always triumphed. In the end our finances became so strained that his visits were cut to twice monthly, and eventually he retired to his semi-detached council house on the Lower Braniel. Sometimes San and I would call on our long walks and she would chat to Mrs Boyd while I tried unsuccessfully to get water out of the heavy metal roadside pump near their house. At Christmas I was delegated to go to Miss Irvine's shop and buy a small block of superior tobacco, wrap it in festive paper and present it with due ceremony. Of the Boyds' private life we knew virtually nothing, apart from the fact that their son was regarded as being in some way not quite satisfactory: from what I could glean it was the 'drink'.

5
SCHOOL – WAR

I must have been about six years old when my mother decided to send me to Miss Fitzgerald's private school in a tall, red-brick semi-detached house at the top of Cherryvalley, not far from the telephone box in which it was said Mrs Allen's husband had been seen doing something of an unacceptable nature. The precise form of his activities was never revealed, but I was told not to engage in conversation with him or accept any offer of sweets. There was much whispered talk about 'poor Mrs Allen'.

By this time I was allowed to go out on my own, provided the destination was known and a time of return agreed. Telephones were not commonly used in those days, so an element of trust prevailed, in that one was responsible for establishing the time and returning home punctually.

Instead of the conventional school satchel I coveted, I had a small orange cardboard attaché-case with metal clips and a brown plastic handle. My mother's belief was that bags worn on the back were detrimental to posture. Logically, I should have thought the converse, but it was several years before an ordinary satchel was purchased, after much pleading. Inside the orange case were a pencil-box with a poker-worked picture of Mount Fuji on the lid, a good selection of coloured crayons, a compass, a rubber, a pencil sharpener, and a range of lovely green-marbled

Venus pencils of different hardnesses. My mother was always generous with art materials, although she drew the line at the oil paints I so much wanted to experiment with. Instead, I had a box of Reeves watercolours, about the cleanliness of which she was obsessive. The box would be inspected on my return home to ensure that the white edges of the little square pots were wiped clean, that I had washed the palette and that the brushes also were clean and tapered to a fine point. She knew well the difference between camel, squirrel and sable, the latter being kept for finest work only. This sort of pernicketiness served to cut me off from the flock even more than did the orange attaché-case.

Later, on graduating from Miss Fitzgerald's to the lowest, coeducational section of Strathearn School, it was the unique cut of my gym-tunic that made me feel like a bird of the wrong plumage. Mother was a resolutely innovative dressmaker and highly skilled with her sewing machine. She had an inexhaustible fund of original ideas for practical dress, and for some reason she decided that a U-neck would be preferable to the square head-hole of the school's regulation tunic. I suffered a lot of derision and hilarity till it was outgrown and I finally argued convincingly for conformity. With the tunic went the obligatory raspberry-coloured woven cotton girdle, which the girls, without exception, pulled as tightly as possible around their waists. The result was that the box-pleats, instead of falling in a straight line from the yoke, cut them in the middle 'like so many sacks of potatoes' in my mother's view. Some of us, even in those days, matured as early as eleven, so the sight of burgeoning bosoms forcing the box-pleats apart was a common one. With unfailing ingenuity my mother measured my natural waist and stiffened the girdle with a canvas backing to exactly that length, so that my tunic fell in the intended way. Little girls derive great pleasure from persecuting the non-conformer, so I was the target of derisory remarks every time it was discovered I was wearing or using one of my mother's inventions. The school tie received the same stiffening treatment as the girdle, with the even greater shame of having a hook and eye fastening at the back, so that the knot would not become worn and greasy with daily re-tying. She always had a point – I will grant her that – but since such details never escaped notice, the mockery continued throughout my early years at school, until competitive interest in the acquisition of 'glamour', and success with the opposite sex, became generally more important than making fun of each other.

A tartan padded cover was fitted to the sharply purgatorial saddle of my bicycle, and there were hand-muffs like small trumpets, made from leather-cloth, fitted to the handlebars to protect my hands in cold weather. A padlock was provided for the bicycle long before theft of bikes became commonplace. Then there were the cotton crocheted toe-covers, which helped to delay the appearance of holes in the toes of stockings. Out of uniform, as she made all my dresses, knickers matched the dress material, whereas those of my contemporaries always clashed. I felt that 'bought' clothes were infinitely superior to those made at home, but I was assured that all ready-made clothing was of inferior cloth, cut and finish.

On the way to Miss Fitzgerald's, apart from keeping a

wary eye out for Mr Allen, I dreaded an encounter with old Mr Dixon and his enormous, lumpen daughter, who wore a tight beige gaberdine coat, buttoned at close intervals, almost all the way to the ground. With this coat she wore a deep cloche hat and shoes with a bar and button fastening: a style of just after the 1914 war. Miss Dixon had a heavy, putty-coloured face, and a long string of saliva dangled perpetually from her mouth. It was said that she had been a missionary in Africa and had contracted sleeping sickness. In hindsight I think she was probably just mentally retarded. Poor thing, she felt driven to speak to children and bent over one with the silvery slaver swinging threateningly ready to strike.

Another local figure remains clear in memory. Austere in the extreme, she wore an almost identical outfit to that of Miss Dixon, except the hat was a wide-brimmed black one, and the footwear neat buttoned boots. Miss Magonigal was a barrister, and reputed descendant of the Drennan family of Glengall Street, who had been staunch supporters of Wolfe Tone and the United Irishmen. She often walked in the vicinity of our school at Belmont and it was clear she regarded children as unfortunate blots on the landscape. She was fiercely forbidding and nobody ever dared to make fun of her, despite the dated clothing.

Presumably Miss Fitzgerald had some qualifications for running a private school, but the class routine was an odd one, due in part to the disparity in age of the children. The desks were miniature and memorably uncomfortable, and all I can recall is copying a picture of the Taj Mahal, learning a few words of French, and doing endless lines of pot-hooks. Thanks to the latter, by the time I moved on to the more efficient establishment recognised by the Ministry of Education in Belmont, I was quite proficient at Vere Foster's copybooks and given to showing off just how speedily and flawlessly I could write, 'Too many cooks spoil the broth.' I believe my stay at Miss Fitzgerald's was less than a year, but I do remember being deeply disappointed at not being allowed to take part in the nativity play. Crêpe paper had been proposed for the costumes, and my mother felt that this, even if worn with the inevitable Chilprufe Liberty bodice underneath, would not be warm enough, so that one would risk getting a chill; and on top of that there was a fire risk.

Strathearn School was ruled by Miss Miskelly, a formidable woman who would have looked like Queen Victoria had she chosen to wear a mid-calf length dress and high-heeled beige kid shoes. Our headmistress had a massive, armour-plated prow and she tapered to tiny feet, like San's sister Molly. She favoured lace at the neckline, and she and my mother palpably disliked each other. The air was full of hostile vibes when I was the not infrequent subject of discussion. I suspect there had been negotiations for 'preferential' fees, which must have been humiliating for my mother. Certainly there was never any question of extras, such as music and elocution, and Miss Miskelly may have exuded some moral censure at my mother's unfortunate marital situation.

There was the incident of the term report in which some perceptive teacher had expressed the opinion that I was a bad mixer. This statement provoked a formal meeting in the headmistress's study, at which she asked me to what I attributed my bad mixing: not surprisingly, I felt unable to enlighten her. Actually by that time I had made a few friends, but all were either a couple of years older or among the less academically inclined from my own age group. I was friendly with two sisters who were good fun and had a garden equipped with a swing, trapeze, and even rings. In addition to these attractions, I felt welcome in their house, where a warm family atmosphere prevailed. Their desiccated grandmother was a permanent fixture beside the kitchen range, where she sat wearing a little lace cap, champing on toothless gums and drinking interminable cups of sugary tea. There were always biscuits of varieties unknown at home, including giant arrowroot, which swelled satisfactorily when dunked. They had smelly spaniels, mangy cats, a marble Grecian figure holding an electric torch in the front porch, and a piano with a metronome on top. The sisters hated the music lessons I so much envied, and never adequately practised for them.

Their parents were doctors and the large house seemed to run itself with the aid of a sole resident maid, whose duties covered everything from cleaning and ironing, to opening the door for patients and escorting them to the waiting room. Loyalty and tact deterred me from reporting the calcified dog turd which remained for months behind the pedestal of the stuffed eagle in the waiting room.

At that time the sense of intellectual superiority that was to inhibit many of my later contacts was latent, so it did not disturb me that my friends' desk work was the despair of most of our teachers, and that we happily shared the back row of the class. In those days a competitive ranking system was in use, and at the end of each week a thin report book giving one's marks in each subject, as well as an assessment of the degree of one's application, behaviour and position in class, had to be taken home for parental signature. How I got away with the suppression of that weekly report is beyond belief. Once the comments were so devastating, and the marks so abysmally low, that I thought it prudent not to take it home for appraisal: behaviour and attitudes left a lot to be desired, punctuality was poor, and written work slipshod. Added to this I had earned two hours' 'detention' at the end of the previous week, and had lied about my whereabouts. My solution to the dilemma was to announce that weekly reports had been discontinued. From then on I had to forge my mother's signature. Incredibly, she swallowed this lie and, as she did not socialise with other parents, was never led to compare notes or remark on the odd change in school policy. By this time her frequent sessions with Miss Miskelly had ceased, but I lived in fear of discovery till I transferred to the senior branch of the school on the other side of Belfast. The forged signatures were patently unconvincing.

I did not really mind being a member of the back row and coming somewhere near the bottom of a class of twenty-five, of which I was, after all, the youngest member. Some of us were conscientious hard workers of average intelligence; others were lazy, complacent and defiant of authority but highly intelligent. My athletic friends belonged to the hard-working, low-achieving group; they never had pencil sharpeners, or if they did, they used them

Four generations, 1896. (left to right) Rosa, Great-grandmother Young holding Dorothy (the author's mother), Grandmother Young

Family group, 1898. Back row: Fred, Rosa, Stonard (Gramp), Gertie (Auntie-Gertie-who-ran-away). Front row: Jo, Grandmother Young, Dorothy (the author's mother), Grandfather Young

Uncle Fred, dressed for a Gilbert & Sullivan performance

Dorothy (the author's mother) c. 1910

David (the author's father) and Dorothy, 4 October 1922

Auntie Rosemary
c. 1928

David Stevenson senior and Eileen (Grandma Stevenson), 1899

Eileen Stevenson and David junior (the author's father) c. 1906

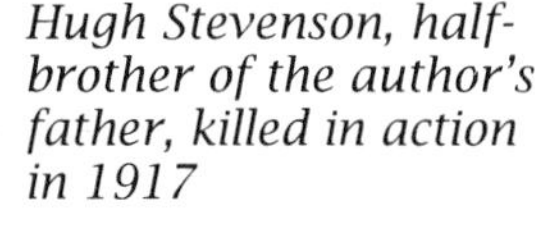

Hugh Stevenson, half-brother of the author's father, killed in action in 1917

David Stevenson senior c. 1919

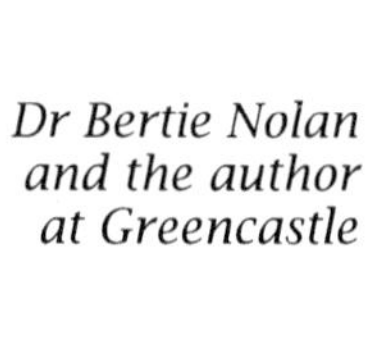

Dr Bertie Nolan and the author at Greencastle

The author at Greencastle c. 1932

The author at Greenisland in one of the straight dresses made by her mother

The author with Auntie Judy

San in one of her wigs!
1972

San as a young woman

The author c. 1948

infrequently. Rubbers, as they were innocently called in those days, were also in short supply and had to be hustled from one desk to the next. Mostly hard, shiny, crumbling and slightly inky, they did not do a good job of erasure. One friend and her sister used to lick a finger and apply it hopefully to the error when no crumb of rubber was at hand; this did an even worse job, sometimes producing a hole in the paper. The technique was calculated to bring out the worst in any teacher inclined to sarcastic exposure of individual shortcomings. The tongues of the finger-lickers protruded in tense little pink points when the labour of writing became too demanding. This habit, allied to their mouthing of each finger-followed word as they went through the agony of reading aloud, did, I am ashamed to admit, arouse feelings of superiority in me. When we graduated to the use of fountain pens, my friends' inkpots were always dry and stuffed with a mixture of blotting paper and chalk crumbs. We were all skilled desk-carvers, using a variety of burins, ranging from penknives to the points of compasses. The engravings could then be coloured, so that the end result was not unlike poker-work.

There were also the joys attached to the use and abuse of chalk. Responsible pupils were selected to prepare a clean blackboard for the start of each class. If the chalk was considered too short it then became the property of the preparer, who also had the privilege of providing a new stick from the supply box in the teacher's desk. As a blackboard artist I was much in demand, but not often so as a cleaner, so an arrangement had to be made with those held more responsible if I were to maintain a regular supply of chalk. Opportunities for exercising one's talent for caricature were few and, inevitably, one would be caught *in flagrante*, possibly with some crude depiction of a teacher, highlighting her less attractive bodily features and eccentricities of dress. Hairy legs, flat-chestedness or the opposite, large feet and any preference for outdated footwear, were favourite targets. I wince today when I think of our insensitive cruelty. We had fine noses for any recently graduated teacher on her first job, a fact often revealed by youthful enthusiasm and the wearing of a too new-looking university blazer.

This was a school ruled by a strict Protestant work ethic, and all the teachers were devout Christian spinsters. It was not till I moved to the senior school during the war that a married woman joined the teaching force. Totally different, she swept refreshingly along those dark brown and cream corridors, her gown and long golden hair streaming behind, her mouth generously lipsticked in a bright shade of orange. Her antecedents were Irish but she had attended an American west-coast university and later married a reverend gentleman, by whom she had several children. She did her best to stir our leaden souls and stimulate our sluggish teenage minds, which by that time were having difficulty in sorting out priorities. For most of us, academic studies and the need to pass school leaving examinations occupied our minds somewhat less than did fantasies about the love lives of those of our teachers who were thought to have any, and our own degree of success in attracting members of the opposite sex. Most of the girls set their sights on members of the Instonians Rugby Club, but I disdained the game and its followers, preferring to go for something more mature. This meant an upper age-limit of thirty-eight. I used deliberately to sit near or beside some pale green, artistic-looking, preferably bearded male in our local bus, and pretend to be deeply absorbed in study of Stendhal, Flaubert, de Maupassant or Dostoevsky. It was not a notably fruitful line of approach, never arousing more than a perfunctory comment.

Religious studies amounted to no more than a couple of what were termed 'Scripture classes' per week. There was a lot of reading aloud as each child, in class order, read four or five verses, with occasional interruptions from Miss McMaster, who would from time to time interject, 'We will leave out the next four verses, please.' Anything to do with adultery, fornication or menses was out but, truth be told, I do not think we were curious enough to enquire the exact meaning of adultery and fornication or, if we were, repeated failure to extract any explicit information had dulled our appetite for enlightenment.

Miss McMaster must have been retained on the staff because she was a truly dedicated and gifted teacher, and she may even have been on the board of governors. She must have been all of seventy in the late 1930s, when she was directing her still formidable energy towards instilling a grasp of elementary mathematics, known as 'sums', and a basic knowledge of the Bible into my group of eight- to ten-year-olds. Scripture classes demanded little but an ability to memorise names, such as those of Joseph's brothers, and a familiarity with the better-known stories. Of the underlying philosophy, ethical and spiritual demands of Christianity, nothing was spoken. I do recall some passing mention of the Crusades and the threat of Islam, but what Islam represented we did not know; indeed, we knew nothing even of the existence of other beliefs and remained stolidly incurious. Morning assembly consisted of a short reading, either by a member of staff or a senior pupil, followed by the singing of a hymn and roll-call, before we scattered to our classrooms. There was the odd diversion of someone farting or fainting, and many of us made attempts to make our neighbour in line giggle so as to earn her a rebuke. Sometimes a courageous rebel would deliberately sing a loud and discordant note or two. The hymns for the most part were incomprehensible then as now, although it did strike me as odd that a green hill should lack a city wall. Like my own children forty years on, I could quite happily sing of what I heard as 'vicious cement' rather than 'fishers of men'.

Miss McMaster's ability to keep order in class was never in question. She was tall, wide-hipped, angular and, viewed from the side, very narrow. Her thin, pure-white hair was savaged back from a high, shiny forehead to form what was more a tight little knob than a bun. Invariably she dressed in a brownish tweed flared skirt, topped by a silky knitted jumper with a low neck filled in with a 'modesty' vest and fastened with a huge cameo brooch. When we infuriated her with our obtuseness, which was often, she would scratch her chest, flat and ridged as a washboard, quite savagely in frustration. Her legs were thin and very bandy, and she wore highly polished brown shoes that laced almost to the ankle: they must have been at least size eight. Nobody ever dared draw a caricature of Miss McMaster on the blackboard.

It was over long division that I was humiliated in front of the entire class. Not in any way gifted mathematically, I had missed the introductory lesson in that knotty piece of 'sums'. I knew, however, the appearance and shape of a successfully worked-out sum and where to put the crosses. Accordingly, I planned to outsmart Miss McMaster by neatly jotting down arbitrary numbers in what I felt were appropriate places, along with the crosses to show that I had taken down a number from the line above. My work looked very neat and I was quaking not much more than usual when called up to discuss my work at her desk. She looked at me piercingly – very like a large bird of prey – before taking one of the purple crayons she alone used for marking, scoring deeply through the paper, slamming the book shut and clouting me on both sides of the head with it, before aiming it at the far recesses of the room, from where I quietly retrieved it amid the delighted, if muted, titters of the class. Thereafter I deemed it prudent to confess if I had not understood something or had missed the introductory lesson.

The daughter of the Very Rev Dr Wylie Blue tried to teach us sewing and 'handwork' as it was called. The antithesis of Miss McMaster, Miss Ailsa Blue was pink and white, soft-skinned and round, and the noise emanating from her class was unequalled by any other. She knew no way of dealing with inattention or deliberate cackhandedness other than to send the offender outside the room. Found by Miss Miskelly, skulking beside a pink and green aspidistra pot in the hall one day, I had to confess to having been put outside for misbehaviour. The hem-stitched traycloth, on which I had been labouring with minimal enthusiasm and over which Miss Blue's patience had finally snapped, lasted me several more terms and was never finished.

Rudimentary lessons in tennis, hockey and netball were given, but techniques and tactics were not the forte of our gym-mistress, who preferred to concentrate on agonising sessions with wall-bars, ropes and the horse. Even today I cringe at the sight of international athletes performing incredible feats on similar horses. Miss Maxwell thought, like the person who feels he will be better understood in a foreign language if he shouts loudly enough, that if she encouraged us stridently we would succeed in somersaulting longways over the horse, whose handles had been removed for this purpose. There were others even less gifted than I who suffered greater agonies during those gymnastic classes. We had one unfortunate girl, a farmer's daughter from the Ards peninsula, whose parents hoped she might aquire some polish at our establishment. She was already well-mannered, but shy and rather too large for her age. She was also obedient to her mother's wishes, one of which was that she should on no account divest herself of a kind of pre-teen corset designed to coax the pubescent female form into the currently favoured adult shape. Miss Maxwell tried all means of persuasion to get Mary to remove the restricting garment, but the battle went finally to headmistress level and Mary won.

If the weather was too bad to cycle, the Stormont bus,

which transported civil servants to the parliament building and passed our school, was an option. The children from Strathearn were not popular passengers, although we were not unruly in any latter-day sense of the word. We threw things occasionally, giggled, ate sweets, kicked seats and were generally restless. I do not know if it was one of my ideas that resulted in a formal complaint being made, but the subject of honouring the school's reputation was made the topic of an early morning address. One of the female civil servants had a hair-do which consisted of row upon row of regular little chipolata-like curls; seated behind her, one could deftly insert tightly rolled, used bus tickets into the interior of the chipolata. Maybe that was the final straw that led to a formal complaint being made to Miss Miskelly.

Sometimes I had to plead with San not to tell my mother, of whom it was San's opinion that I was 'scared stiff'. This was said objectively, for she and my mother respected and liked each other. It was with San that I most often heard my mother laugh, although San's total inability to understand the functioning of the simplest bits of domestic machinery often aroused my mother's impatience. Vacuum cleaners were particularly liable to play up in San's hands; there would be a faint burning smell, and clouds of dust would surround her and the machine, while she complained, 'This old thing's at it again!' My mother would come to the rescue and find some indigestible item, such as a hairpin, stuck in the rubber belt, or discover that the bag was patently in need of emptying. The gas-poker for lighting our temperamental coke-burning stove in the kitchen was another tool which conspired against San. Its rubber tube would get kinked or the holes from which the gas was supposed to jet would be blocked, many matches would be used and a pervasive smell of gas would creep from the back regions of the house. The question of which knob controlled which burner on the cooker was one which troubled San till the end of her days, and she got markedly more confused when we changed to electricity.

I was a sneaky little coward, too proud and secretive ever to confide in my school friends. If ever there was a problem to be solved, I had to deal with it unaided. Never did it occur to me to ask for an outside opinion, and this attitude later landed me in deep trouble. Headstrong and glorying in defying conventions, I cut a swathe through life and sometimes through people. My mother used to remark bitterly, 'You and your grandma would ride roughshod over anyone, trampling their feelings into the ground.' These words echo freshly down the intervening years, along with 'He's far too good for you' (apropos my husband), 'Your aunt's in one of her huffs again', but most often 'Just like your grandma.'

Accordingly I agonised over what to do about an invitation to a birthday party to be given by a friend I really liked, and to whose party I very much wanted to go. Admittedly the friend's mother was somewhat bizarre, but not so much so as to justify my mother's attitude, which was to boycott the entire family. I never felt free to ask this girl to visit our house, although I went to hers if I felt certain my mother would not find out. The invitation had demanded RSVP, so I was well aware that a written reply was required. Not being up to this, I embarked on a tissue of complicated lies as to why it would be impossible for me to be there.

I was confused and saddened that such a nice girl could have such a dreadful parent, and also ashamed to find that I quite enjoyed talking to Mrs Flett when I did manage to sneak a visit. Their house was almost back to back with ours but a lot larger, and the proximity added to my embarrassment. It was furnished rather sparsely in Art Deco style. Mrs Flett was an admirer of Carmen Miranda, and modelled her appearance on that of the film star. Lots of lipstick, a whitely powdered face, jet-black hair done in a severe Spanish style, long, curved, shiny scarlet nails and gypsy earrings completed the effect. Paradoxically, she came from old Orcadian stock and spoke with a strong, albeit 'refayned' Scottish accent. I suspect she regarded me as being quaint and 'old-fashioned' – a euphemism for precocious. She was undoubtedly curious about my mother's married status, the whereabouts of my father, and any other information she could elicit. We had discussions about such things as marriage and childbirth, and my views on the latter caused much hilarity, when I admitted I was afraid the baby might get stuck in my tubes. We also talked about health and nutrition and I was naive enough to reveal my mother's adherence to the Hay Diet. I loyally tried to explain the theory behind the non-mixing of proteins and carbohydrates in the same meal. Slow to learn what topics were bound to provoke widespread ridicule, I also let it be known at school that we were on the Hay Diet.

Mrs Flett kept an unfortunate goldfish in a bowl that

sat in the centre of the dining table. No rock, sand or weed enlivened his shiny globular prison and I predicted his early demise. Meanwhile our own fish were constantly developing fungal spots, turning belly up or showing disorders of balance that required treatment in running water or baths of potassium permanganate. Mrs Flett's fish was in seemingly rude health during my last visit to her house.

There was a Mr Flett, a seldom-seen, plodding figure with a briefcase always in hand: I have no idea what his job was, but it involved lengthy absences from home, and it was rumoured that his wife consoled herself with the company of a retired sea-captain when the opportunity offered.

Mother's attitude to all parties that were announced as being in celebration of a birthday was that this displayed a deplorable lack of breeding on the part of the parents, and grasping tendencies in the child. So, when it came time to mark my own birthday, I was forbidden to say for what reason the party was being held. The ordeal took place once only, the outbreak of war thankfully putting an end to such frivolities. There not being sufficient surplus from the weekly food ration to make the sickening cakes and biscuits normally served on such occasions, my mother escorted a small group of carefully vetted invitees to the Picturedrome cinema in Mountpottinger to see Anna Neagle and Anton Walbrook starring in *Victoria the Great*, and thereafter to eat a high tea at the Country Tea House in central Belfast. No doubt she thought the film would be educational and therefore open to no criticism as regards choice by the guests' parents. However, the tastes of my peer group ran to the musicals of Deanna Durbin and Judy Garland or the comedies of Abbot and Costello, the Marx Brothers and Laurel and Hardy. The latter were – and remain – by far my favourites, but culture won the day. I recall no fissling of sweet papers, munching of popcorn or other normal childish behaviour. I hope my mother enjoyed it: she remarked when the last guest had been deposited home, 'Well, that's off my chest.'

Chamberlain's broadcast announcing that a state of war existed between Britain and Nazi Germany, remains, like the assassination of Kennedy, clearly in my memory. My mother was sitting beside the elaborate beige-and-orange tiled, typical 1930s fireplace in our sitting room when he came crackling over the air from our brown bakelite wireless set. She was so moved she told me to go away: I suppose she did not want me to see her crying. It was, after all, only twenty-one years since the end of the Great War, in which her fiancé had been killed just four days before the armistice was signed.

School routine changed in that there were air-raid warning exercises, we had to carry our gas-masks everywhere in their little cardboard boxes, and there was gas-mask drill. This provided us with the opportunity of making vulgar trumpeting noises by applying the snout of the mask to the cardboard box. There were various patriotic appeals, one of which requested that we turn in all our aluminium saucepans to make bodies for Spitfires; we were warned that 'Careless Talk Costs Lives' and exhorted to 'Dig for Victory' and not to spread VD.

With absolutely no concept of what war really meant,

despite artists' lurid impressions of battles of the past in our history books, I believed that soldiers went into battle wearing red jackets and busbies. The mundane khaki uniform of the private soldier, increasingly seen in our neighbourhood, was a distinct disappointment. My mother listened avidly to all BBC news and encouraged me, as she had done as early as the Spanish Civil War, to find the places mentioned in the atlas. Of human suffering, senseless mass destruction, shattered lives and futures, I thought not at all: not even when we were urged to feel grateful to the men of the merchant navy who were ensuring our food supplies.

The silver barrage balloons that floated over the docks at Sydenham were attractive to children, and I remember in the hot summer of 1940, while the Battle of Britain was at its height, hoping for the thrill of seeing an enemy aircraft. Grown-up opinion, however, held that Belfast was too distant a target for the Luftwaffe.

When my mother began to dig an air-raid shelter in my aunt's back garden – our own being too full of rockeries – I thought this was yet another of her cranky ideas. She dug down into reddish clay and made quite a deep shelter with little niches for the candles. Sadly, it slowly filled to mid-calf depth with water before she got the corrugated iron roof firmly into place. When the raids did come, in 1941, we sheltered under the stairs and occasionally went out to see what was happening when the sounds became more distant. One could hear the explosions and see the night sky lightening momentarily, and there were places where a sinister red glow began to grow in intensity. The searchlights were active and I remember praying, as much as I had ever prayed about anything, 'Please don't let them get him - he's such a long way from home.' I knew these sentiments would be regarded as unpatriotic and kept them to myself. The Germans apparently pasted the Antrim Road part of Belfast in mistake for the docks, but a few land-mines and incendiary bombs did fall in the Castlereagh hills. That was the nearest most of us got to the violent reality of war.

There was a large army barracks at what is now the headquarters of the RUC near Knock railway station. Little girls behaved in provocative ways even then, and some of us would linger deliberately in the vicinity of the entry gates where a sentry was always on duty, hoping to engage in casual chat. They were mostly Cockney family men, lost in this almost pastoral, outer-suburban community. I remember one of them taking the handlebars of the bicycle on which I perched, one foot on the ground, and moving it to and fro, remarking, 'Oh, so you know what that's all about do you?' I did not but was sensible of some vague sexual undercurrent, which satisfied me that I might not, after all, be entirely unattractive to the opposite sex. These flutters were not without the risk of being reported either at school or at home, as the barracks was almost opposite Lizzie Lynn's newspaper, tobacco and confectionery shop, and Lizzie was one of San's main sources of neighbourhood gossip.

If none of us 'got into trouble', it was more by good fortune than anything else. Our mothers spoke vaguely of things nice girls neither did nor permitted to be done, but they were unspecific. It was said that 'No nice man wants shop-soiled goods', and in mid-teen rebellion I commented that nice men were mostly dull, and who, in any case, cared what their preferences were?

Strathearn was, at that time, a junior school. One sat, at the age of fourteen or fifteen, an examination known as the Junior Certificate for Northern Ireland, so at the height of the war the school was well-stocked with nubile young girls, eager for they knew not quite what. Some were sexually precocious, wore lipstick out of school hours and had tunics shorter than average, displaying a variety of shapely legs, sheathed, if they were fortunate enough to possess them, in fine cotton lisle rather than wool. One or two brazen specimens bleached their hair and sported the ultimate in sophistication – a permanent wave. We favoured a hairdresser in Chichester Street whose cutting was inspired, despite the fact that he made us uncomfortable by enquiring if, by any chance, it was 'that time of the month', because if so, the permanent would not take so well.

At prefect level, some of the girls had begun to go out with boys and would regale the less mature among us with details of their experiences. There was talk of erections, although this was not the term used, and 'not going the whole way'. But as I was three years younger than my two closest friends, it was not until I moved to the senior school that temptation to go *any* of the way arose.

Moving to the senior school involved quite an early start, as a bus had to be taken to the centre of the city, from which one walked to school, if time permitted, so as to save the one and a half penny fare. If not, it was a tram from opposite the City Hall to the grim, grey stone building that was Victoria College, situated where the University and Lisburn Roads divide. The cheerless edifice was built on a narrow triangular plot between the railway and Lower Crescent; there were no attendant greenswards and our playing fields were some distance away. It was an airless building, the ground floor of which housed the assembly hall, the headmistress's office, the kitchen and the dining hall. At basement level were our lockers, a row of insalubrious lavatories, hair-clogged basins with spotty mirrors above, and the gymnasium.

On the way to the bus to central Belfast I had to pass Alfie's property, which was the neighbourhood affront; Alfie was well aware of this, taking a certain perverse pleasure in the fact. Some tried to ignore the eyesore, although this was hard as the bus stopped right at his front gate. Gate it had once been, but it had been long ago nailed up, the main entrance being round the side, leading through a littered yard to the back door, where Alfie mixed messes in a clanking bucket and Mrs Alfie yelled at the kids. They were numerous and all roughly the same size. I suppose the older ones stopped growing while the younger ones got enough sustenance slowly to attain average height. All had straight, straggly black hair, ashen faces, snotty noses and stick-like legs. The overall impression was grey, and it was said that they and the O'Shaughnessy brood were a sore trial to the headmaster at Gilnahirk Primary. No toy graced the yard, although a rusted tricycle rested in a corner beside the remains of an iron bed.

Alfie could be depended upon to surface from whatever mess he was stirring to greet passers-by with the typical Ulster jerk of the head that constitutes a greeting. I am convinced that he enjoyed the discomfiture, particularly of young girls, that the sudden appearance of his turnip-like face under its greasy 'duncher' provoked. The face was reminiscent of the Halloween turnips we carved – slightly purplish, with uneven stumps for teeth. Maybe he was 'digging for victory' as the government exhorted us to do, but somehow his crop yield never looked healthy. At all times of the year there were small, limp cabbages dangling sadly on the end of long, curved stems, and the ground never had the well-groomed appearance that advertises good husbandry. Any failure was surely not due to lack of manure; indeed, a regular hazard of passing the gate was to pick one's way through the gobbets of dung that had dropped from Alfie's orange and blue cart in transit to his manure heap, which was not far from the back door and the kitchen window.

The top end of Alfie's property was divided by a high cypress hedge from that of Miss Gaussen, a lady of venerable Anglo-Irish lineage who lived in genteel impoverishment with her two Sealyham dogs. Despite the hedge, Miss Gaussen was unable to disregard the proximity of Alfie and spent much time and energy trying to rally neighbourhood support to 'do something about him'. The final fuse was blown when Alfie decided to keep a few pigs. An effective protest was made, after which the pigs disappeared and a miscellaneous hen population with ruling cock took over to scratch around among the cabbage stalks. Naturally there were complaints about the cock's crowing, but the hens actually laid enough eggs for an 'Eggs for Sale' sign to go up, and some of the more charitably inclined bought them in the hope that it might help Alfie's wife, who was patently in need of extra funds. From time to time a mangy dog skulked around, tail between legs, apprehending the next kick from the boot at the end of a heavy gaitered leg. There were miserable splodgy kittens too, but nobody liked to report these facts to the 'Cruelty' lest it should add to Mrs Alfie's problems. I never heard happy laughter coming from the house or yard, and it was rumoured that there were beatings on Saturday nights. One day an ambulance came and Mrs Alfie, who had a persistent cough, was not seen again. The children survived a few months of Alfie's care, then the 'For Sale' notice went up. Now the house has the same respectable suburban appearance as the others in the road but its garden is enviably larger than most.

The precocious girls already approaching school-leaving age were objects of envy and endless speculation for us younger ones. Some of the seniors were even permitted to attend the Saturday night dances at the Plaza Ballroom or, at a somewhat superior social level, in Thompson's Restaurant in Donegall Place. By this time the US army had established bases in Northern Ireland, so I reckon any parent allowing a daughter to attend either of these venues was either innocently unaware of the 'goings on' or hoped their offspring would join the ranks of the early GI brides. One of our less academically inclined, blatantly bedworthy seniors did just this and disappeared from the scene forever amid much conjecture as to what the outcome of having 'done it' regularly on Saturday nights might have been.

Needless to say, I was not allowed to attend dances at either the Plaza or Thompson's, so had to confine my outings to the sedate 'hops' held at Miss Foster's. Here, because there was no bar, the admittance charge was low and it attracted a less adventurous type of customer. Sometimes a uniformed male would appear and, no matter how insipid, he would always be assured of female interest. We sat on benches around the walls in the way common at country dances, the lights were never dimmed and one was sure not to miss the last bus home.

For a relatively small community, we had more than our share of retired missionaries, one of whom was Mrs Toner, who lived on her own not far from San. My ears must have been constantly on the alert for items of gossip deemed in some way unsuitable. Accordingly I amassed a smattering of half-truths. I got the impression that the late Mr Toner had either been unable to perform his conjugal duties or been slaughtered in China very shortly after having first done so. Whatever the truth, Mrs Toner had a strong antipathy to sexual activity of any sort, and there was a regrettable tendency for the adults to snigger when her name was mentioned. With the arrival of the US troops in Ulster, Mrs Toner formed a vigilante group that patrolled the grounds of Belfast City Hall at night, torchlights in hand, spotlighting some of the intimate acts performed by the soldiers and their local pick-ups on the benches or the grass. I gathered it was possible to 'do it' in quite a number of surprising positions. One soldier took exception to being spotlighted and resorted to physical violence. Mrs Toner's pince-nez had to be replaced, and she wore an arm in plaster for a while. After that incident no more was heard of the vigilantes, so I suppose they confined their efforts to prayer.

Despite my preoccupation with sex, I was terrified of flashers, as at that time it was not recognised that for the most part they are inadequate, pathetic creatures, unlikely actually to put to use the weapon they display. One man used to thrust his engorged penis through the wire netting surrounding Belmont Tennis Club, and another revolted me on the bus one day by strap-hanging and fondling his parts, just at my eye-level, under his raincoat, which had a convenient slit pocket. The friend I was with was incredibly obtuse when I insisted on getting off one stop short of the one agreed.

Campbell's Coffee Shop, opposite the City Hall, close to the Linen Hall Library, was frequented by most of the minor literati, artists, actors, BBC playwrights, teachers from the Royal Belfast Academical Institution, some of our own more adventurous teachers, and eager theological students such as Ian Paisley. There was also a small coterie of Jewish international bridge players. Paisley, the bridge players, junior architects and the early members of the Belfast Arts Theatre favoured the first floor, while the BBC and schoolteachers preferred the ground floor. After school a few of us would foregather on the first floor to spin out mugs of the thick, beige-coloured fluid that passed for coffee and, if finances permitted, eat one of Campbell's famous bacon and mushroom rolls. The atmosphere was smoky and somewhat steamy: particularly repugnant on wet days, when raincoats and umbrellas added to the general fug. The tables and chairs were red Art Deco vintage with tubular steel legs, and the walls had been decorated by Rowel Friers with cartoons of renowned local characters. The ambience was as near Bohemian as I could find in the Belfast of that era. There was, of course, a scattering of earnest young accountants, trainee bankers and mill managers, but I found them dull and preferred to lurk on the fringes of the groups of aspiring theatre directors, art film enthusiasts and minor poets and painters.

We should have been easy prey for any calculating man whose intentions were less than honourable, but, with the exception of the elderly bridge players, none of them tried to take advantage of our vulnerability. This group relentlessly pressed invitations for us to come for evening lessons in bridge to some shady address in Duncairn Gardens. Eventually I think their egos got bruised by our increasingly transparent excuses for non-acceptance and the atmosphere became less cordial. Some of us spent the mid-afternoon hours in Campbell's rather than applying ourselves directly to the load of homework which was our daily lot. Lolitas one and all, we wore our berets at provocative angles and were liberal with the lipstick. I was spotted by our maths teacher and reported to the headmistress as having been seen made-up and wearing the regulation school beret at an angle like a French film star. The reputation of the school was once more at risk.

The embryonic Reverend Ian Paisley held court among the intense students of the Presbyterian Training College, and periodically mugs would bounce on his table as he thumped a point home with his fist. We kept our distance from this scene but had no idea that here was a politician in the making.

Of Irish politics I knew nothing at all. The history of Ireland was taught as a separate subject in our school and, like sex, one gathered it was something too complex and emotive to be studied in any great depth. I must confess that I found the unending list of uprisings, mostly, it seemed, led by one or other O'Neill, boring in the extreme. The myths and legends were, I suspect, regarded by our teachers as something too akin to the Celtic dream and so, like Irish folk music, their study smacked of republicanism. Gradually I came to sense something of the tensions stirring in the province and caused more unease at home by loudly voicing my anti-royalist sentiments and my belief that an Ireland united was the only sensible solution. Of economics and the power and influence of the Roman Catholic Church I remained oblivious.

6
After the War

Our straitened financial circumstances made it impossible for me to study medicine but I was in any case so immature that I would undoubtedly have been an early dropout. Nonetheless, a year was wasted trying to attain the levels required in physics and chemistry for admission to the faculty of medicine. I enrolled in the first year university class in mechanical engineering, lectures for which took place in the flea-ridden College of Technology in Belfast. I learned virtually nothing, lacking the groundwork the rest of the students already had. A thoroughly mixed bunch we were – a few earnest females who later went on to teach science in private schools, some equally dedicated, hard-working male students, and a few clever disrupters of the class. One of these, a particularly repulsive Lothario, knew no other line of courtship than to sneak packets of Durex into my handbag: for some reason I felt guilty about this.

Who recommended that I might benefit from taking this course, I do not remember, but presumably an enthusiasm for the subjects and a determination to work were taken for granted: in this they were labouring under a major misapprehension. I had been frustrated in my wish to join the WRNS by my mother, with whom the argument that with the navy I should be trained for a profession and receive free board and lodging did not outweigh her fear that I would be all too easy prey for unprincipled naval officers (see 1948 diary). Running away to join in defiance of parental objection was never a serious option, but I was resentful and became even more vehement in my disdain of the social and ethical behaviour patterns deemed proper, and which, my mother warned, would be defied at a cost. Unmindful of what the neighbours may have thought about her own pursuits and interests, she clearly applied other standards where my activities were concerned. I suppose she felt that any transgressions of mine would be seen as emanating from her failure as a parent. My only lasting reproach on that count is that I was offered no spiritual guidance and, in consequence, grew up in a sort of vacuum. Even now I find it impossible to understand my mother's almost total rejection of religion, her emphasis on affairs temporal and her failure to recognise that some basic knowledge of what it was one was rejecting was fundamental to any sound education. San was no great respecter of men of God either, although she was a believer. In her final years she attended church in one of the small seaside towns of the Ards peninsula and left a legacy to the church, the young minister having hinted it might grease her way through the holy gates. Towards the end of her life my mother too became more tolerant, and received, with moderate graciousness, the dutiful calls of the local minister, who came from Derry and knew something of the family history.

To marry, as I did in 1950, a non-believing German of mixed Jewish-Catholic parentage in a Presbyterian church was an act of ignorant confusion. The misgivings of the minister, a pupil of my husband, were scarcely hidden, although we had previously gone through a painful afternoon of 'examination' with him.

It having been generally agreed that there was no money in the pursuit of art, having decided against medicine for a variety of reasons, and there being at that time no faculty of archaeology at the Queen's University, I drifted into an apprenticeship in the photographic business of a family friend. A premium of £500 was paid, from which my wages for three years was to come. I got thirty shillings a week for the first year, three pounds for the second and a handsome five pounds in the third year. Calculating this now, I see the friend got a very good deal indeed: free labour and a five-pound profit over the three-year period. It was a totally unbusinesslike arrangement, typical of my mother, and Lionel was not really qualified to train anybody, being no more than a gifted amateur himself.

The premises were cramped and insanitary, the dark-rooms primitive and our processing methods open to criticism, as laboratory conditions did not prevail. We did, however, give personal attention to the processing of amateur films and to their subsequent printing. This was done on a variety of papers ranging from linen-textured ivory to sepia velvet. The main profits came from industrial photography, a few weddings, at which none of us was much good, some child portraits and quite a lot of work involving the reproduction of old photographs, paintings, sculpture and *objets d'art*. It was at this time that my interest in buildings and architecture was first aroused. Shortly after the war, the Council for the Encouragement of Music and the Arts (CEMA) organized an exhibition of Georgian architecture and our firm was invited to travel all over the province, recording some of its rich heritage of early nineteenth-century, eighteenth-century and even older houses. We used an old mahogany and brass plate camera with a rising front, which would now be a museum piece. To erect this camera with its tripod in a street, focusing under a black cloth, was not my favourite job, as it was a sure mirth-provoker with the local louts. Often we had to go to take pictures of mill machinery in such places as the Belfast Ropeworks or Mackie's Foundry. I remember the choking fibre that caught in my throat and covered my clothing. Like asbestos and coal dust, these fibres must have done irreparable harm to those who daily worked in that throbbing, clattering atmosphere.

There was a sliding metal grille between the entrance to our studio and the street, and it was my job as apprentice to clear this of the night's detritus, which was mostly nothing more unpleasant than greasy chip wrappings and the odd bottle. Being of a frugal disposition, the boss did not employ a cleaning woman, so it was also my duty to vacuum and tidy the reception area and straighten the fussy little crushed velvet mats his wife had made to protect the tables. We displayed old copies of *Photograms of the Year*, the *Art of Photography* and other journals, in which a few daring nudes were to be found. It used to amuse me to surprise some of our respectable elderly male customers studying these in close detail, often swiftly turning the page or feeling constrained to make some remark as to the aesthetic merits of the picture.

Many local artists and quite a few Jewish refugees from central Europe were among our regular customers.

Considering their relatively small number, the latter made a lasting impression in the fields of music and painting in this largely uncultured backwater. Zoltan Frankl was of the same build as the late Robert Maxwell and had a similarly overpowering presence. His attempts to make himself understood in English never got beyond the most rudimentary and this angered and frustrated him. I used to wither under the force of his reverberating attempts to communicate an often complex idea, and feel guilty that I was not quicker in the uptake. The incident of the 'fax meal' was typical, and I was slow to realise that it was a facsimile of the original he wanted.

Paul Nietsche came too, wanting pictures taken of his heavily black-outlined, ferocious fruit pictures: he was prolific but I have not seen one of his works outside the municipal art gallery since his death. The Hammerschlags enriched our local orchestra: Heinz and his wife Alice both played the violin. Alice was also a gifted painter and a pioneer in the use of acrylic paints. Colin Middleton sometimes came, but he was disappointingly distant, not to say gruff, and slightly intimidating, wearing at all times of the year ancient leather sandals. Ashen pale, with an angular countenance reminiscent of an early Tudor portrait, and painfully diffident, John Luke was a regular customer and brought his lovely *Virgin and Child* to be photographed in the tempera stage before he vulgarised it with too much crimson, blue and yellow where gold was indicated. This painting subsequently perished in a fire somewhere in Armagh but I kept a print of the underpainting.

Of the local artists, Langtry Lynas was our most

regular caller, although he did not really qualify as a customer. He would talk endlessly about the new technique he was trying to perfect – pointillism really – and how difficult this was going to be to reproduce satisfactorily, but we were seldom actually entrusted to photograph one of his works. What he really enjoyed was having another port of call after he had exhausted his welcome, and Mr Vitty's patience, at the Linen Hall Library. Langtry was less than five feet tall and quite frail in body, if not in voice, by the time I met him. For everyday wear he invariably had a tailor-made suit of pepper-and-salt tweed, a matching overcoat with a little cape, and a deerstalker hat. His accessories were a stick for gesticulating with and a foul-smelling pipe. He would sit for hours in one of our armchairs behind a screen of smoke, listening to discussions with customers and offering unsolicited comment from time to time, often startling people who had not noticed the source of the smoke.

Langtry enjoyed the morning coffee break, in which I included him, but my boss did not quite know what to do about his too frequent presence in our front room. On the one hand he was slightly flattered as, after all, this was an artist of some repute; on the other hand, the 'tone' Langtry lent to our studio was not widely appreciated. Langtry's combinations stuck out greyly at his cuffs and at the bottom of his trouser turn-ups, and he had a convenient theory that too much washing was bad for the skin. 'My skin cleanses itself,' he once told me. This was patently untrue, as his hands and nose were speckled with small, black, grease-filled pores. His little hands were purplish and swollen and his finger joints badly deformed. Painting was becoming increasingly difficult, but he always had a new theory and something new in mind, if not already on canvas. He lived on the Upper Newtownards Road just above the Arches and used to speak of his wife, with neither affection nor respect, as 'she' who was instructed to lay his meals on a tray outside the attic room that was his studio, entry to which 'she' was forbidden. He had sons, one of whom rejoiced in the name Dante, and he spoke with evident affection about him.

Another of Langtry's ports of call, though more difficult to reach as he had to take a tram from the city centre, was the Belfast Museum and Art Gallery. There again feelings were mixed when he hove in sight. John Hewitt was curator at that time and suffered considerable embarrassment when Langtry attended an exhibition opening. He would make audible and mostly disdainful comments on the paintings currently on display, and sometimes slanderous remarks about their perpetrators. He was automatically invited to all such ceremonies, as some of his own work was on display in the museum's permanent collection. For any formal occasion Langtry would wear his better outfit, which he had prevailed on Mr Stringer, who ran a tailoring establishment in Bedford Street, to make for him. The new topcoat was made of a rich, purplish-brown soft velour cloth and had a black velvet collar to go with his velvet skull cap. The collar was always liberally scattered with the dandruff that fell from his long white hair. Mr Stringer accepted, more or less resignedly, that payment was likely to be by widely spaced instalments.

Sometimes Langtry would get as far as Smithfield market and the secondhand bookshops of that part of town. After a rewarding visit he would come to me waving his latest purchase, often a Blackwood's school classic edition: Plato, Sophocles, or odd things like Maeterlinck's *Blue Bird*.

Of his antecedents he never spoke, any more than he alluded to the bad times when he had been reduced to painting lampposts for the Belfast Corporation. It was rumoured that his mother was Lily Langtry and his father possibly Edward VII. My last memory of Langtry is of a tiny figure toddling slowly across Donegall Place, directly in the path of an oncoming trolley-bus, waving his stick and shouting, 'Ye can all just wait!'

The belief that our family was somehow 'different' and by implication superior to the common herd, can surely not have been entirely my own invention. My mother's attitude to schoolwork was that we were all so bright we did not need to stretch ourselves inordinately in order to 'get by'. Inherently intellectually lazy in any case, I deduced from this that to 'get by' was acceptable, and accordingly developed few academic ambitions. This attitude would have been alien to Gramp's philosophy and must, I fear, have emanated from Rosa. On the other hand, Gramp had held that education was, to a large extent, wasted on the female, as she would inevitably marry and find fulfilment in her domestic role. My mother, as evidenced by her many school prizes, had been a potential academic highflyer, leaving school in 1914 at the age of eighteen. At that time it would have taken full parental backing and great determination to enter university, which is clearly where she belonged.

Almost inevitably I embarked on an unsuitable relationship with an officer in the Royal Canadian Navy, a married man eighteen years older than myself (see 1948 diary). Of course, most of my friends had already guessed that he was married, but I found out only when one of his junior officers tactfully explained that our evening date would not take place because Harry's mother-in-law had just died in Plymouth and he must attend the funeral. I think I managed to conceal the shock, but I remember the concern in the eyes of the news-breaker, who was probably disgusted to see his superior officer 'taking advantage of an innocent young girl'. Deluded that this was the love of a lifetime, I continued the liaison for some time, making myself boringly unavailable to other more suitable sniffers around the perimeter fence, so to speak. Naval duties, the discipline of letter-writing, and my successful pursuit of another equally unsuitable man, finally brought the affair to an end. He tried to revive it a few years later but there was nothing left but an awkward gulf in communication. He regretted seeing me having 'thrown myself away' on a middle-aged refugee, whose politically active father had fled from Berlin in the early 1930s.

The officer is now dead. Many years later I wrote to the naval headquarters in Ottawa to establish his whereabouts, only to be informed somewhat pompously that 'This veteran sadly passed away in 1974.' My motives for wanting to write to him were not, in any case, the best. I really wanted to let him know that, despite his predictions, I had not made a total mess of my life.

EXTRACTS FROM DIARIES 1941, 1948

Author's Introduction

Twice only over the years did I complete my resolve to fill in a daily diary. Attempts prior to 1941 fizzle out feebly with such statements as: 'Went to school' or 'Forget what did.' So what was the catalyst? One could hypothesise that hormonal changes had something to do with it, as I record, with evident pride, the growing-up process and the onset of menstruation (having clearly mugged up the spelling and informed myself rather more fully of the facts of life than could be done by reading the Lilia sanitary towel leaflet). I know precisely what triggered the 1948 resolve when I read the first entry. It is clear that I am suffering from a crippling hangover, although unaware that the consumption of large quantities of rum and Coca-Cola during the New Year's celebrations might be the cause of my malaise. I had also experienced my first orgasm and lost my virginity (in that order!). I am appalled that in the 1941 diary there is no mention for some months of the fact that the country is at war. I appear to have been totally preoccupied with mundane everyday events. Possibly there was a deliberate attempt to insulate me from what was going on, although as I was clearly addicted to radio comedy and the 'pictures', current events can scarcely have evaded my notice. Gas-mask drill and evacuation of the school premises, not to mention all windows being decorated with a crisscross of sticky tape, and the attendance of both my mother and San at the primary school ARP classes to learn basic bandaging and first aid techniques, must surely have made some impression. There is little mention of food, clothing or the shortage thereof, and I do not remember ever longing for any particular item. I was vaguely aware that men of the merchant navy were undergoing perilous passages in order that the population should not go without some essential imported goods. My feelings had been mixed at the start of the war when my mother refused the kindly-made offer from distant cousins in the USA to take me as an evacuee. I clearly recall that at the time of the outbreak of war it was my belief that all soldiers wore red jackets and busbies. I appear to have been an extraordinarily unimaginative child in many respects.

DIARY 1941

JANUARY

Wednesday 1

Went to the circus – it was extremely good, especially the acrobats and tight-rope walker. Miss Hind [ex-missionary from China, sister of Bishop Hind] asked me to dinner [probably lunch] on Saturday. Went to Miss Ferguson's and had a good tea. It snowed a little so I hope it will snow in the night. [I remember Miss H clearly, though only from the time she had turned a sinister waxy-yellow and had retired to Donaghadee to die.]

Thursday 2

Went to see *Green Hell* with Douglas Fairbanks and Joan Bennett – it was very good. It didn't snow in the night: I was disappointed.

Friday 3

Went to Dickie's [younger son of Bishop Hind. He was a wholesome boy of thirteen, whose main interests were wood-turning, experimenting with his chemistry set and researching the possibilities of polaroid photography] had a good time. It still hasn't snowed. I am still disappointed.

Sunday 5

Had a superb time skating at Brookmount. Met Dorothy [most promising young skater of whom I was jealous] who had broken her leg. The fountain in Lisburn had icicles on it.

Tuesday 7

Went skating again and took tea. Auntie [my mother's sister Rosemary, thirteen years her junior and only eighteen older than me – then a civil servant at Stormont] brought her dinner and ate it in the car. Had a good time. Grannie [my paternal grandmother, with whom my mother was on cool terms] came up tonight.

Wednesday 8

Went and met Grannie. [She always installed herself in the Royal Avenue Hotel during her quarterly visits to Belfast from Derry.] She gave me an old Bishop's ring and a scarab, and gave mother earrings. Very nice too. Lord Baden-Powell died in Kenya.

Friday 10

Went to San's, she gave us a very good tea and we talked. I finished the third of Mrs Whitfield's brooches today – one more to do. [Ghastly felt-work cut-out flowers in the then fashionable colours of petunia, pinks and blues, with safety-pin to attach to the lapel of one's 'costume'. Mrs Whitfield was one of San's succession of lodgers, a massive blonde of uncertain age who came from Lancashire and was working at what was locally referred to in some awe as the 'listening station', situated behind barbed-wire security gates at the top of the Gilnahirk hill. It must have been a telecommunications centre.]

Monday 13

Started lessons. [This was the year my mother kept me at home, teaching me herself, after a battle of wills with the headmistress who had to be convinced (a) that I was 'growing too fast' and (b) that my mother was fully competent to undertake the job. When I returned to school it became apparent that she had been more than competent, to the ill-disguised chagrin of Miss Miskelly.]

Thursday 16

Went and saw *The Great Dictator*, it was awfully good. [I find this statement odd, as I knew little or nothing of politics, or indeed what the war was all about. In fact I remember being bored, but as I was not writing for anyone else, I suppose it must have appealed in some way.] Had fish and chips and cabbage and a bottle of milk at Woolworths - nice.

Friday 17

Went for a walk with San - snow still lying. Saw Ian, he was not much better. [Neighbours' child, some years younger than I.]

Thursday 23

Did more work on Eileen's flower. [Eileen, three years older than I, was for some years my 'best friend': an odd association of which more later.]

Monday 27

Did lessons. Nearly finished my knitted pixie-hood which looks very nice indeed. My tail bled again worse luck.

Wednesday 29

Tail stopped bleeding. Finished my hood. Coughed a lot.

Friday 31

Stayed in bed but did Arithmetic. Took ephedrine, it made my heart go funny.

February

Saturday 1

Mother didn't let me go to drill. Went up to see San. She brought home the Pinocchio book - it is lovely.

Sunday 2

Drew and copied drawings from Pinocchio book. Auntie came to tea. I fried the pancakes.

Monday 3

Did lessons. Went to knitting party and talked. [This is weird: I regularly attended parties of middle-aged women who were knitting a variety of sometimes misshapen items of clothing for 'our poor boys', anything from balaclavas, through mittens, scarves and socks. What my contribution to the talk can have been I dread to contemplate. The group met at Mrs Hind's house, so here was the possibility of encountering the romantically unpromising Dickie – whose ears were even more a feature than those of Prince Charles – and eating homemade cake. It was probably in this house that I first became enchanted by Chinese forms, as the bishop had collected jars and old wood-carvings of ancient sages with domed, shiny heads and flowing beards.]

Tuesday 4

Went to see *Rebecca.* Nora came to be tried on. [My mother was ekeing out her meagre income by using her considerable dressmaking skills. I, to my discredit, was ashamed of this.] Mrs Hamilton came to choose her pattern. Her dogs yapped.

Friday 7

Went into town and got lovely white boots and a difficult

puzzle. Had dinner [lunch] at the XL – delicious. Did lessons. AM came in the afternoon. [Annie, another girl to whom I had sworn eternal friendship. Like Eileen, she was three years older than I, stringy where E was juicy, and she later declined into an anorexic state, which eventually killed her at the age of twenty-seven. The disease had no name to us at the time and we were appalled when she was admitted to a mental hospital and force-fed.]

Saturday 8

Went to drill – very strenuous. [I loathed it – why am I not saying so? Probably fear that my mother might read the diary.]

Monday 10

Did lessons. Went to knitting party. Felt horrid there, had headache and shivers. Went to bed.

Tuesday 11

Didn't sleep at all last night – have temp. of 102. [Writing here very shaky.]

Wednesday 12

Much better. Finished *Ballade in C Minor*, it was good. Read more of the *Big Six*. Got up for tea.

Sunday 16

Read a lot of *Rebecca*, listened to *The Taming of the Shrew*. Auntie came to tea.

Wednesday 19

Saw *Elizabeth and Essex* – they mucked up the history, but the costumes were gorgeous.

Saturday 22

Caught a flea – must have got it in the bus yesterday. Went to tea at Auntie's. Got the brush for the Frosts' stopped up sink.

Tuesday 25

Did lessons. Rang up station master at Lisburn, he said he would tell us if there was skating. Went to Mr McKeag [orthodontist] and got new thing on my band.

Wednesday 26

Went over to Kincraig [local doctor's house]. There was a nice kitten. Ginger [our inbred dachshund] made a pool on my mat in a hysteric.

March

Wednesday 5

Did lessons. Met Eileen at the Astoria and saw Boris Karloff in *Black Friday*. Very good. Eileen came to tea. I like her. [This friendship continued till E's marriage in 1948, after which predictably we drifted apart. E was no intellectual, to put it mildly: she was also unashamedly anti-Semitic (although I did not understand her scathing allusions to anyone with Gold in their name) as well as anti-Roman Catholic, and referred to anyone she regarded as being lower down the social scale as 'these people'. She developed an affected manner and voice, and shamelessly cultivated anyone remotely aristocratic. She was in her element when she joined the WRNS at seventeen and worked for Lord Kilmorey on *HMS Caroline*. There were many romances and an hysterical time when she was twenty-one and thought she might be 'left on the shelf'. This preoccupation became conversationally boring but came to an end when she married Redmond, a much older divorcé. 'Older men are so much more reliable.' Clearly a father figure, he was a pleasant man who had been to Oxford, was financially comfortable and socially well-connected. She bore him many children and became increasingly preoccupied with her 'position' and her large house with velvet curtains and cretonne covers. By this time I was voting Labour, voicing my opinions on free love, and ostentatiously reading the *Manchester Guardian* and the *Listener.*]

Thursday 6

Did lessons. Had tripe for dinner. Ugh. Went to dentist, he let me off for another six months. Nice. [Ultimately it was far from nice; he was a short-sighted, kindly old soul who let small cavities become large enough for him to see to fill them. When I finally changed to another – known locally as 'Butcher' Elliot – there were about sixteen teeth to be attended to.] Had tea at Mrs King's. Went for a scramble up the hill to see the foal.

Wednesday 12

Mother told me some more Facts of Life.

Sunday 16

Re-potted Auntie's plant in our big flower pot. Went for a walk up the hill with Auntie and Norah. Our marmalade turned out well. We got 10lbs out of six oranges and one lemon. [These will have been sweet oranges – a rarity. I do not recall the recipe in detail but there would have been shredded carrots, a little sugar and a lot of gelatine to make it set.]

Monday 17

Had holiday [St Patrick's Day]. Went in to Ian's and kept him out all morning. He came over to our garden and said what for? [He rewarded me for my childminding by chasing me with a large worm of which I was terrified.] Got Mrs Frost some cigs and she gave me some of the peppermints. I did Auntie's hair for the matinee.

Thursday 20

Did lessons. Went to Louisa's [local home bakery] to get provisions for tea. Flo came to tea. [Friend of my mother who owned horses and repeatedly broke her collarbone – very elegant on a side-saddle and equally so in the evening dress that my mother was making for her at the time.] Rang up Eileen – we are going to *The Invisible Man.*

Friday 21

Did lessons. Went to pictures with Eileen. She came to tea. Am going to learn golf with her. Johnny is coming up from Dublin. [Johnny had been engaged to Auntie for a very long time: he was a few years younger and a graduate of Trinity College in Dublin. He was also a Jesuit-educated Roman Catholic and his parents thoroughly disapproved of the alliance. At this time he was probably already serving in the army and home on leave. He always referred to me, with a modicum of affection, as 'The Brat'.]

Monday 24

Did lessons. Johnny not coming for three weeks. Went to Frosts for a bit. Have a cold I think. It rained all day.

Tuesday 25

Stayed in bed. Mother went riding. Read *Little Women* again. Fell downstairs on my back – all the way.

Wednesday 26

Cold much better. Ginger had two fits. Eileen rang up – she had a cough. Our daffodils are nearly out.

Friday 28

Had lessons. Went to see *The Blue Bird* – it was very good but not as good as *The Wizard of Oz.*

Monday 31

Did lessons. We sunk three Italian cruisers and two destroyers – good! [This is the first mention of war apart from ARP and gas-masks.]

April

Tuesday 1

April fooled Mother by asking her to clean up one of Ginger's pools in the hall. Went to see the Frosts and gave Mrs F the recipe for meat roll. We have captured Asmara – Hip hooray!

Sunday 6

Gave Auntie and Mrs Frost some daffodils. Gardened and ponded [annual mucky clean out] in afternoon. We have captured Addis Abbaba.

Tuesday 8

Had an awful time with air-raid and could not get to sleep.

Thursday 10

Poor Scamp [Frosts' dog] is dead. Went to see Annie, she is looking better. E did not come as two people not allowed. [This may well have been a hospital visit at the time AM's weight was down to five stone four ounces.] Grannie came to tea. Gave Annie daffodils.

Wednesday 16

Did not get to bed till five am cos of awful blitz. Auntie had to be fetched from Stormont with chill. Went over to

San's and gossiped. Played with Ian.

Thursday 17

Am thirteen. Mother gave me a lovely soap tray and 2/6. Auntie gave me 5/- and a scarf. Mother went in the afternoon to see evacuated people. Winnie and Billy are coming to sleep. [These were the niece and nephew of our maid, whose family lived in the vulnerable area of Sydenham near the docks.]

Saturday 19

Winnie and family slept here. [This meeting was not all I had hoped for in a social sense, as all were crippled with shyness.]

Friday 25

Went to shops for oranges. Went to see *Dr Cyclops* – very good trick photography. Helen came to try on frock.

Tuesday 29

Still have a cold. Did a lot of my jumper. We are evacuating Greece. Hope I shall be better enough to see *La Mort de la Cygne.*

May

Friday 2

Cut two lawns and played with Ian a wee bit. Bill [tortoise] began to eat again. Johnny came at seven-thirty and I stayed up till ten.

Saturday 3

Johnny slept in our dining room in a sleeping bag on a li-lo. He took lots of photos. J is engaged to some girl who has a pash on him. [This indicates that his long engagement to Auntie R is over. The girl with the pash was the general's daughter, whom he subsequently married.] Did gardening for Mrs Frost. Had tea at Auntie's.

Monday 5

Had another air-raid and stayed up till four. Water has to be boiled. Siren again at one. M went to ARP post – reconnaissance we think.

Tuesday 6

Had another air-raid – not so bad. Played with Ian. Had two sirens. Got sausages for Mrs Frost. Mother got sand-bags.

Wednesday 7

Had another air-raid but not a bad one. Am very sleepy. We are looking after AM's canary. Went over there for tea. Mother got more sand-bags.

Thursday 8

We shot 23 Jerrys down last night. Had no raid thank goodness. Gave purple sprouting broccoli to Mrs Frost. Mother went into town. She got me frock stuff, knickers and hankies. Nasty cat has got the birds [the nest I had been watching daily]. San gave me a bit of parachute cord. The billeting man came but we already have the Barnes family.

Friday 9

Had another warning. Went to McBride's shelter – not nice. Eileen rang up to ask me to tea in town. Refused. Went into town – the wreckage is horrible. Packed valuables for country.

Saturday 10

Had another warning. Went to shelter again and sniffed and coughed. Cut two lawns. Played with Ian. Mother took things to country. [Where? I have no recollection: possibly to Auntie Judy's in Lurgan.] Johnny arrived and I stayed up till ten.

Sunday 11

Got up late and bathed Toby [baby tortoise]. Went for a short run up above Mr Warwick's and gave the dogs a good walk. Johnny had tea with us but then had to go. Ginger ran away twice. Thirty-three Nazis shot down.

Tuesday 13

Hess landed in Scotland and is in hospital with a broken ankle. Gave Ian purple sprouting broccoli. Went to shops – got 6/- savings stamps and a lettuce.

Wednesday 14

Did lessons. Mother went to town. Poor Mr West is dead. [Eileen's father, who was found drowned after going for a walk along the seashore.] He was so nice. Poor Eileen. Mr Boyd came [my mother's patient gardener]. Gave more sprouting broccoli to Mrs F. Lent Ian *Peter Pan.*

Tuesday 20

Got postcard from Annie – she will be home tomorrow. [Probably after incarceration in a mental hospital in Armagh, where she had been force-fed.] Got films but they had been kept too long and were fogged. Cut lawn and edges.

Saturday 24

Tea at Auntie's – lettuce and chocolate cake. We have lost *HMS Hood*, worse luck.

Tuesday 27

The sweep came – he could not find anyone else to want him. [This was a mountainous, laboriously breathing man we called 'Yus' because that was his most frequently heard utterance. He lived in a minute house - now long demolished; probably a gate-lodge dating from the late eighteenth century - near the junction of University and Lisburn Roads.] We have sunk the *Bioma*. Hooray! Going to bed early again cos of state of bedroom. Mrs Whitfield came with her dress material.

JUNE

Sunday 1
Wore frock - it is nice. Went for a picnic to Sheeplands [near Ardglass]. It was glorious. Auntie and I bathed - it was not as cold as it has been sometimes. Came home late at 10.30. Drank more milk. No lobsters.

Wednesday 4
Did lessons. Mrs West and Eileen came to tea. I like Eileen. We sat in garden then took them home [to Craigavad] in car. We picked up an air-force man. Up till 10.15. [Mrs West became a wartime replacement teacher after the death of her husband, although she was so dim we could not believe she had actually got a degree. On record is her thoughtful reflection, 'It's funny them being black and us being white.' What she did share with my mother were painful recollections of living with a man addicted to alcohol.]

Friday 6
Got up late. Did lessons. Played with Ian and made him a lovely sandcastle then the little pig kicked it to bits. I scraped lots of cake basins. Mother went to ARP.

Sunday 8

Got up late. Auntie made up my face and I looked grown-up. Sat in garden. Listened to *Trilby*. Saw Ian. Hosed and watering canned Auntie's lawn.

Tuesday 10

Did lessons. Eileen rang up to ask me to go to pictures. We went and it was a scream.

Saturday 14

Packed to go away [to spend the weekend with Grannie in Portrush]. Set off at eleven and arrived at one. Had nice dinner. Went to Mrs Frizell's and she came out to tea. Gerald is a funny little boy. [No recollection at all of these two.] Went to Marie Ross's. She makes lovely things with felt and gave me a pin-cushion. Grannie gave me stamps. Mother sent me to bed early. I cried. [They probably wanted to discuss my father's death, which took place in Worthing in 1940: cerebral haemorrhage as a direct consequence of his drinking.]

Sunday 15

Nicer day. Breakfast early – bacon and eggs. Down to caves with Dandy [hotel dog] and into the kiln. Went to church in turban. [Turbans of the Rita Hayworth/Carmen Miranda type were 'in' at that time, but it must have looked unsuitable on a child.] Had chicken for dinner. Went to Portstewart and saw people. Salmon for tea. Went for lovely scramble with Mother.

Monday 16

Lovely day. Up at 7.30 for scramble with Dandy. Took lots of photos. Had patties for dinner. Took photos of Grannie. Took more photos of Giant's Head. Left for home, worse luck.

Sunday 22

Got up late. Read *William* [Richmal Crompton]. Cut up rhubarb for jam. Helped Auntie with her deck chair. Germany has marched into Russia. Winston made a speech – awfully good.

Monday 23

It rained a bit. Went up to San's and cleaned her lodger's floor. Ate cake and got peppermints. Read *William.* Listened to *Monday Night at Eight* and a programme on ballet. Stayed up till 10.00. Knitted.

Tuesday 24

Lovely day. Jimmy Millar is missing. Poor San and Mrs Millar. [Jimmy was Molly's only child, an RAF pilot who disappeared without trace over Sicily.] Cut grass. Got postal order for Aunt Jo [older, spinster sister of my maternal grandmother Rosa. Lived in Newcastle-upon-Tyne and got income support from my mother and Auntie R – who could ill afford it]. Went to Kineda [small local tennis club] with Auntie – it was nice of her. Could not play.

Saturday 28

Made almond cheese cakes. Auntie's birthday – gave her a book. Went to tea at her house. She got chocolates. Mother was lovely and kind and bought me blue stuff for a summer coat.

Monday 30

Got up late – holidays started. Played with Ian – his grandpa was there. Mother made me eat awful junket – horrid. Finished Auntie's net. [Snoods were the fashion – probably that.]

Wednesday 2

Woke up at 5.30 am with a headache. Have light sunstroke. Took aspirin and felt better. Went to town and arranged about a hat to match my coat. Shivered after dinner and went to bed.

Sunday 6

Got up late. Cut grass. Ian came in and I played with him. Made plasticine model of Venus de Milo. Auntie came to tea – played ping pong.

Wednesday 9

Tore my stripey frock on the window frame. Met Grannie in town for dinner. Met Mrs Malcomson and went to tea there. Lovely place. Mr M gave me some bird's eggs and a blower. Saw Grannie off on train. [The Malcomsons were Quakers and lived in a secluded house with a large garden. Mr M would now be an 'offender', as he had a huge collection of birds' eggs. He also had an extensive cactus collection, which endeared him to me.]

Tuesday 15

Played with Ian. My frock was not ready in time to go and meet Eileen. Had tea at the Country Tea House. Got Star-Sylko for Auntie. Mr Frost's foot is fractured.

Saturday 19

Got up late. Went to shops. Got chocolate and fly floppers. Played with Ian. Went to tea at Auntie's and contradicted her about Susan [her dachshund] so was sent to bed early.

Sunday 20

Got up late. Read *Orange Blossoms.* Made sponge cake for

Auntie – it looks OK. Played with Ian a lot – he was cross. Auntie came to tea and I apologised. Susan had no worms to be seen. Went to bed at 9.30.

Tuesday 22

Got up latish. Played with Ian a bit. Went down to Eileen's and played tennis. Had a nice tea and went for a short walk along the shore. Left at 9.15 and in bed by 11.30.

Wednesday 23

Mr Boyd came. Rang up Annie and asked her to play tennis. We played a bit in the afternoon but she had to leave at 4.45 – I stayed till 5.45. Ma would not let me go back again.

Tuesday 29

Got up late. Had egg for dinner. Went up to San's and helped her to get dinner for the lodger. Had a fine argument with him. Wore yellow satin evening shoes. Started to knit gloves in Star-Sylko.

Wednesday 30

Rang up Eileen to wish her a nice holiday. Mother went into town to get buttonholes done. I had dinner alone. Made beetroot and white sauce and custard and pineapple. Went up to San's. Mrs Millar was there – helped get supper.

August

Friday 1

Went into town and met Eileen – gave her the parcel. Had coffee at Robinson & Cleaver's. Left her at bus – said goodbye. [Clearly I have a crush on E, although I have no memory of anything other than markedly heterosexual thoughts.] Went to Reid's and saw two weaver birds for

10/-. Thought over buying them. Bought them, they are nice – Pip and Squeak.

Saturday 2

Got up late. Played with Ian. Birds are OK. Auntie went to have dinner with Johnny who is up for the day. Went to tea with them – had tinned herrings – nice. Played Ten-bad-min-is [badminton played with tennis rackets].

Monday 4

Auntie has a holiday. We went into town. Mother met Flo and had tea. Auntie and I had milk shakes and rolls. Auntie bought a hat and I said it was like a Jerry – she was very cross. [Auntie was embarking on an affair of sorts with a professional golfer and subsequently decorated said hat with artificial flowers for some special assignation. The relationship did not last.]

Wednesday 6

Got up late. Mother went into town. Played with Ian a lot. Scraped cake basins in Mrs Frost's. She gave me two cakes. Andersons lost their budgie and I helped chase it – we did not get it. Auntie has a bad cold.

Sunday 10

Got up late. Auntie got up for dinner – played cards and made a seven storey card house. Played demon patience – it is fun.

Thursday 14

Annie's sister has TB. Poor Annie, I am so sorry for her. Went into town and got nail polish, comb and orange stuff. Had milk shakes. Met San. Jimmy was last seen in a dinghy but it disappeared. I think there is still hope.

Saturday 16

Set off for Ballycastle – it rained on the way but was a lovely run. Did not much. Had tea and went to bed at 10.00 pm. Went to shore a wee bit.

Sunday 17

Wet morning. Went along the cliffs before lunch. Found ruined castle. Had tea and stayed up till 10.15 pm.

Thursday 21

Did a lot of work [preparing for return to formal school]. Met Eileen in town and had tea at R&C's. She said Dougie nearly put his arm around her. Left her to the station. [Dougie progressed rapidly from that stage and they indulged in heavy-petting sessions, of which I was given a fair account. 'Of course, we didn't go the whole way.']

Friday 22

Got up late and did more work. Went to San's and asked her to come for a run in the car. She came and brought sandwiches and lemonade. Gave two soldiers a lift. Frosts are back.

Saturday 23

Worked. Mother went to the shops and I made the dinner. Rice and cheese and beetroot. Played with Ian. Sat in the garden – it was a nice day.

Sunday 24

Got up late. Took Patsy [San's dog] up home as she was fighting with Susan through the gate. Drained the pond. Ian came in and was a bally nuisance. He was disobedient so I sent him home. Winston made a speech – it was good.

Thursday 28

Am going back to Strathearn – worse luck. Went to Annie's new house, it is not bad. She took me for a long walk in the pouring rain. Laval was shot – condition critical.

Friday 29

Mother went to see Skelly [Miss Miskelly, headmistress of Strathearn, with whom my mother had a very prickly relationship]. I am to go back on Tuesday and have exams – worse luck. Arithmetic, Geography, Drawing and English. Went up to San's and got tomatoes – did her nails with a nice colour I mixed.

SEPTEMBER

Monday 1

Got up latish. Did a lot of work on Arithmetic. Made custard. Went to San's. Saw Mrs Taylor – she is funny looking. Did San's nails and did Mrs Millar's too. Also did her face – it was improved.

Friday 5

Had English and Drawing. Drawing was easy and English not bad. Eileen arrived early which was good. She invents stories in bed too. I think that is great. She stayed till 8.15 pm. Went for a short walk. I kissed her goodbye.

Monday 8

Went to school. Have passed my exams thank goodness. Asked Skelly for marks and she said all I should know was whether I had passed or not – old bitch. Did French homework.

Tuesday 9

Went to school. Skelly relented and said I got quite good marks. Had History – Miss Hawkesworth is nicer than I had thought she was. Went to dentist – he drilled and it hurt.

Wednesday 10

Went to school. Went to Hinds with Mother. Poor Mickey Hind is missing. [He had been married a few weeks previously.]

Tuesday 18

Went to school. Asked Skelly about dancing, it is 42/- for October to Easter. Got afternoon off. Went blackberrying with San and got a lot. Saw Aurora Borealis.

Saturday 20

Went into town to meet Eileen for coffee. Left her at train. Made jam and got 9lbs. Poor Annie's sister died last night.

Tuesday 23

Finished Geography in bed. Did not much. Adair child ran into me and broke three spokes and buckled the front wheel. Took it to the bike man.

Thursday 25

Went to school. Got the half day off because the others had Domestic. [My mother claimed that this was a waste of time, money and ingredients and that all could be picked up at home – I tended to agree with her for once.] Met Eileen at Ritz cinema and saw *All This and Heaven Too.* It was excellent but very sad. Did homework. Am never in bed till 9.30 pm now.

OCTOBER

Wednesday 1

Had singing. I am in the choir! [They lived to regret it.] Had games. Cycled a bit with the others. Joy was back.

Thursday 2

Went to school and afterwards to the pictures – it was awfully funny. Flo came to tea with some lovely stuff to make an evening frock. [I remember it clearly, black net with a sprinkling of iridescent pink flowers for the skirt, and a black velvet top.]

Wednesday 8

Did not go to school. Had dinner at R&C's. Grannie disgraced us by cooeeing down the lift shaft. Had tea at the Country Tea House.

Friday 10

Mother went into town and gave Grannie dinner. She gave me another drawing block and a mapping pen. I stayed at home cos of cold. Mother left her at the station. Auntie passed her medical board for the WAAF.

Sunday 12

Got up terribly late. Auntie huffed cos I said she poked her head when she talked to Mr Wadell. She came to tea.

Wednesday 17

Went to school. Did not get detention. It poured.

Tuesday 21

Went to school and had dancing – nothing much new. Took Miss Watson into the Arches [junction of Holywood and Newtownards roads – my mother must have taken the car]. Went to Mr McKeag's and he put an awful looking gate across the front of my teeth.

Thursday 23

Went to school. Mother picked me up at dinner time. We had lunch in the XL – very nice. Went to Disney's *Fantasia*. It was exquisite, especially the fairy bit with the frost. I picked up my bike on the way home. Finished my jumper, it is lovely.

Sunday 26

Got up very late. Played patience a lot. Tidied up Auntie's box room and saw a piece of Grannie Young's wedding dress. [This was Rosa, who was married in 1894: her mother had decreed that a white dress was a waste of money and insisted on a maroon silk with beige lace trimmings. The choice was a cause of lifelong resentment. The waist was minute – about twenty inches I should guess. I still have the lace.]

Monday 27

Went to school. Won 5–0 against Bloomfield Collegiate. I did not play well. Lelia rode up beside me on her bike and ran into me. Cut my knee and stocking. Am sore.

November

Saturday 1

Dug a drain in Auntie's garden away from the back door. Went to San's. Mother brought home two lovely budgies – green and blue. Had tea at Auntie's.

Monday 3

Holiday and got up late. Went to pictures with Dickie. *The Thief of Bagdad* with Conrad Veidt. It was excellent with some marvellous trick philosophy.

Tuesday 4

Went to school and had dancing. We did some hard Russian steps or wiggles. Did homework. Auntie was called up.

Wednesday 5

Went to school. Had match against the blues – they won. Both our budgies died. One because we think he ate too much – the other looked quite healthy.

Sunday 9

Auntie has to sail on Wednesday. I helped to clear space to put her things in our attic. She gave me some drawing blocks and came for last Sunday tea. We had crayfish and cake.

Wednesday 12

Went to school. Had a match which we won 4–2. Left Auntie at the boat – it was awful saying goodbye.

Friday 14

Had hockey practice. Got sent to bed early cos of untidy room. Eileen rang to ask me down at the weekend.

Thursday 20

Went to school. More people rang up about my train. One came at 4.00 pm and bought it for £5. [Pity about this – a nice Hornby set that would fetch a fine price now.] Susan was dosed for tapeworms.

Sunday 23

Got up late and did my English. Our little weaver bird had a bath. It is not like Sunday without Auntie. Her house is let to nice people called Quintrell.

Friday 28

Went to school and did not get detention. My coat is finished.

Saturday 29

Coat is lovely. Met Eileen in town for coffee. Got a nice lipstick for 2/–. Went to the pictures in Holywood with

Joan and Cecil. I wore a turban and lipstick.

Sunday 30

Stayed the night with Eileen. Went for a walk. Eileen is in fits because Dougie is leaving. Mother called for me in the car.

December

Tuesday 2

Went to school and had dancing. We have to do a display at Xmas. Arith and French exams tomorrow.

Thursday 4

Had Algebra and Geography exams. Algebra was terrible. Got 43% for my arith. Went to see *Bitter Sweet* with Nelson Eddy and Jeanette McDonald – it was extra good.

Friday 5

Had English composition and Drawing – neither of them was bad. Developed a streaming cold during Drawing. San came to tea. Went to bed early. Got only 29% for the Algebra.

Saturday 6

Stayed in bed. Got letter from Auntie yesterday. She has been moved to a nasty place [somewhere in West Yorkshire I think]. She may get leave soon which would be great. Flo came to tea. [Flo used to infuriate my mother by leaving a genteel bit of butter on the side of the plate: considering the weekly adult ration was two ounces, this was a bit insensitive.]

Sunday 7

Got up late and had a nice roast for dinner. Read up Shakespeare and do not want to be better for tomorrow as it is English literature. We and the USA are now at war with Japan.

Monday 8

Had to go to school – worse luck. Had the English lit which was not too bad. Was able to quote Shakespeare. Hawaii was bombed, there are three hundred casualties.

Friday 12

Auntie came today at lunch time which was good.

Saturday 13

We all went into town and had soup at the Milk Bar. Ginger still has a few worms. Went to tea at Mrs Quintrell's.

Sunday 14

Had our Xmas dinner [early, because Auntie had to leave before Christmas Day]. Boyd gave us a lovely fowl for 6/6. Xmas pud was nice too. We all slept.

Wednesday 17

Went to school. Had singing. It will be awful on Friday.

Thursday 18

Went to school and rehearsed play. Helped put up Xmas decorations. Made a felt flower for Miss Knox.

Friday 19

Went to school. We did nothing till 10.30 am. Then prizes were given. Concert started. Our play was OK – singing not!

Sunday 21

Got up late and didn't do much. Caught a mouse last night. They are trying hard to get into the aviary. Mother made a nice sponge bag for Grannie. Got some lovely silk stockings.

Wednesday 24

Got an awful book from Norman [who owned a bookshop

in Derry]. Eileen sent me a nice book. San came over with her presents – 2/6 for me and chocolates for Mother. Mrs Millar gave me a bar of choc.

Thursday 25

Very quiet Xmas – the first one without Auntie. Mother gave me olives, stockings and a book. Boyd gave us a hen which was very kind and he got his usual bar of tobacco. Mrs Frost gave me bath salts and Annie 2/6.

Friday 26

Stayed in bed in the morning and finished Norman's lousy book. Had a headache but got up for tea. Mrs Hind asked me to go and see *When Knights were Bold.*

Wednesday 31

Am still asthmatic but got up and did a lot of Grannie's calendar [a laboriously copied pen and ink drawing of a Thames river scene]. Grannie is coming up next week. Poor Mr Sam is dead. Mother played for me in the evening – she plays beautifully.

Diary 1948

January

Thursday 1

Felt terrible when I got up – only three hours sleep. Didn't have any breakfast to speak of. Everyone at work similarly affected except Lionel [boss] of course. Harry came in just after lunch to see how I was. Came home for tea and then up to the rink. Comm. Pears insisted on taking me home – very awkward, conversation didn't flow. [Harry's superior officer, who may have had reservations about the previous night's celebrations.]

Friday 2

On the mend again I think, face still very rough though. Rang up Harry to ask him out on Sunday. Wasn't going to skate but he persisted so I went. He took me home in the jeep after the dance interval, but wouldn't come in as he had to leave it back at the Belgravia. [One vehicle shared among senior officers, many of whom were billeted at this hotel.]

Saturday 3

Home for lunch. Had to stay in and not go to the pictures with Harry as Margaret [skating coach] came out in the afternoon. Heard all about her holiday in Davos.

Sunday 4

Harry came out for tea. George McK [retired maths teacher who coached me through university entrance exams] came out later and they seemed to get on well together. [George came from County Clare and Harry had early ancestors from Ballinasloe.] Harry brought a marvellous cake sent by his sister in Canada.

Monday 5

Got an awful book out of the library by Salvador Dali which I shall change as soon as poss. Went up to Dr McLaughlin about my nose. He said it was not the same as Auntie's and cauterised it immediately. It wasn't too bad apart from the padding. He removed a humiliatingly large piece of wax from one of my ears.

Tuesday 6

Bitterly cold again. Tea in Campbell's and then up for [skating] rehearsal, now I'm incorporated in an inefficient quartette which includes Sheila S who is mentally deficient. Harry has gone on sea trials till Friday.

Thursday 8

Very late in and got the same bus as Lionel. Had to take pictures of signs on the Albert Bridge and got frozen.

Saturday 10

Lousy day – Harry got back last night and took me out for coffee in the morning. Had lunch at the Café Royal with Auntie and Mother. Met Harry at 5.30 and had a meal at the Imperial. Went to see *Duel in the Sun* at the Ritz – very bad taste, quite enjoyed it!

Thursday 15

Very late in and coincided with Lionel again. Got a nice skirt length in Cleaver's, also the bit of satin for my top. Margaret rang up about 5 to say Mother had broken her kneecap and had gone off to the RVH [Royal Victoria

Hospital] with Auntie. Went to see Mother who seems OK but worried that they haven't set it yet. Auntie couldn't sail either. [She had started a high-powered secretarial course in Oxford on discharge from the WAAF.]

Wednesday 21

Got in fairly early for once. Mr Boyd came about manure and I had to pay him. Auntie in for lunch and she went to see Mother. I was to have taken Harry, but we decided not because Mrs Walker [notorious gossip] might be there. Busy doing a complicated composite photo. of Courtauld's Factory at Carrickfergus. Came home for tea and started in to my skating dress.

Friday 23

Another cold day. Eileen came in to see me – told her to collect her birthday present tomorrow. Harry came in just before 5 with a film. He is going to Derry tomorrow to get a few clothes. [Ready access to tweeds from County Donegal and a more relaxed attitude to clothes rationing than prevailed in Belfast.] Came home and finished my skating dress – skirt seems too short.

Monday 26

Lousy day – rained all the time. Auntie and I went up to see Mother at the Alexandra [nursing home] – not terribly prepossessing outside, but very comfortable inside and she is getting well fed.

Wednesday 28

Lovely sunny day. Lionel took me down to the Public Records Office with the Recordak [microfilm] machine, and we photographed some of the Drennan letters. [This job took us a long time. The Drennan family, strong supporters of the United Irishmen, had lived in Glengall Street at the end of the eighteenth century. The letters were riveting reading, a fact which delayed the page-turning and protracted the job.] Very cold again but it all looked a bit better. Went to see Mother.

Saturday 31

Fairly busy all morning. Lunch in the Café Royal with Auntie and then up to see Mother. Came home intending to do a lot of washing but Harry rang up and asked me down to the Châlet. [This was the most fashionable 'nightspot' of the era, in Crawfordsburn Country Club.] Called for me and brought a dozen eggs. Had a good time and joined another party of six. Got his life story on the way home. [A heavily expurgated one I suspect.]

February

Wednesday 4

Went up to see Mother – a few disapproving remarks about my 'affair'. Up to the dance club. Harry took me home in the jeep.

Friday 6

Lousy day – wet snow all the time. Auntie went skating – had to get her to bring in my fur coat it was so cold. [An appallingly unflattering garment made of slabs of grey rabbit 'coney' in which I looked gigantic but felt sophisticated.] Met Eileen in Eva Clarke's buying a hat. Auntie and I went to see Mother who is being allowed home tomorrow. Harry didn't ring till 8 – very disgruntled that I can't go out tomorrow.

Monday 9

Lunch with Eileen in the Rainbow – still further instalments of the epic. She asked me officially to be a bridesmaid and hopes to be married in April. Went up to the figures club. Coffee with Harry in Sherie's.

Wednesday 11

Miserable day. Got very wet at lunch time. Met Margaret and Eileen in Campbell's. Hairdresser at 3 and didn't get out till 6. It looks awful and inclined to frizz so I evolved a new style with a knob at the back and up at the front. Tried to get in to see *The Birth of a Baby* but there were long queues. [That was about the height of sexual voyeurism in those days.]

Saturday 14

Got to the GC [Grand Central] about 8.30 and had a lovely dinner and danced till 12. Margaret got on all right. Got home at 2. Mother very wakeful and Harry went after 4. [Mother's bedroom was on the ground floor and somewhat too proximate to our sitting room!]

Sunday 15

Felt lousy but got up to feed the cats. Recovered a bit round lunch time. Spent an unprofitable afternoon talking the matter over with Mother and Auntie. Curse arrived last night.

Tuesday 17

Busy all day. Very cold. Went up to rehearsal: Harry and Barbara there. Came down in the tram with him as far as Shaftesbury Square. [His digs were on the Stranmillis Road, so this was the natural parting of our ways.] Further lecture from Mother on my morals etc. Danger of playing with fire etc., etc.

Wednesday 18

Tried to ring Harry but couldn't get through. Doctor came to see Mother and told her to walk as much as possible. Came home and did the ironing, washed stockings and darned. Usual discussion re my affairs went on till after 12. Auntie very awkward. [In retrospect I can see that she may well have felt somewhat jealous as Harry was about the same age as she, and I was leading what seemed to her a hectic social life.]

Sunday 22

Met Harry and saw *King of the Turf* at the Imperial with Adolphe Menjou – very sad but not extra good. H gave me a huge box of chocolates.

Monday 23

Not an awful lot to do. Had lunch with Margaret and did a bit of shopping. Eileen brought me some coupons and I bought a pair of gloves 18/9. Up to the club – Harry and Heather there – he took us both down and left me home. Serious 'conversation' on the way.

Tuesday 24

Barbara, Harry and half the RCN [Royal Canadian Navy] seemed to be up at the rink, including his padre. Much annoyed as I shall have to miss a cocktail party on the ship tomorrow. Had two tangos with Margaret and fell heavily on my rear because of Harry tripping me.

Wednesday 25

Sneezed a lot in the morning and stayed in ironing hankies till 10.30. [Not an unusual occupation in those days.]

Saturday 28

Not much to do at work. Eileen came in to see me about 11

and we went out for coffee. [Her fiancé] Redmond's family are giving him a birthday party tonight which seems to be aweing her a bit. [R's mother was a diminutive but very formidable Bostonian, who patently disapproved of her son's second choice. His father, on the other hand, readily succumbed to Eileen's unsubtle but undoubtedly succulent charms.] Met Harry at 4 and we went to see *Dear Murderer* with Eric Portman and Greta Gynt - very ingenious and well produced. We had dinner afterwards in the Grosvenor Rooms - salmon and a lovely trifle. [I was finally catching up with Eileen's blazing trail: she had been dining there three years previously, and I had been very envious.]

March

Monday 1
Auntie came into town with me as she wanted to queue for wool - got some nice white stuff. Went up to the figure skating club. Harry there and took me home in the jeep - awful remarks made when I got in at 11.

Tuesday 2
Bought some marvellous stuff for an evening blouse - Mother thinks it is awful. Harry brought me some Kleenex hankies - couldn't take me home as he had only the open jeep.

Saturday 6
Met Harry at 4.30 and we fed at the Café Royal. Saw the Adelphi Players in *Eden End* by J. B. Priestley - very good.

Sunday 7
Didn't do much. Harry came out for the evening. Played

draughts, Peggity etc. – quite hilarious.

Monday 8

Mother got a letter saying Gertrude Stevenson had died (TB). [GS and family owned the Drumaweir Hotel referred to in the Inishowen chapter.]

Saturday 13

Went to Price's re frocks only to be told they were sold. Harry rang to say he could not get any transport for the evening, so we went to the flicks, *Personal Column* and a Laurel & Hardy – quite good. Chicken supper afterwards.

Wednesday 17

Busy all day contact printing. No reply to Lionel's ad for a new assistant yet. Ordered a plait of hair at Rottgers – 4+ guineas which seems a lot. [It was real Italian peasant hair.]

Thursday 18

Two girls in to be interviewed by Lionel. One about 6 feet tall and rather tarty – the other seemed quite nice though married. Went up to the dance club. Asked Harry out for tomorrow night.

Monday 22

Fairly busy all day. Got a violet blue Jaegar utility dress – very new length – looks marvellous on. Great weight off the mind. Came home for tea. Eileen rang up apropos bridesmaids' dresses. Went to the AGM of the Ulster Skating Club – Mother wasn't re-elected thank God. Very dull and wordy as usual. Held in the Carlton – they gave us quite good grub for a shilling. Wore my new dress and created a stir.

Saturday 27

Glorious day. Went shopping in the morning with Mother.

Got up to the Boat Club [more of a tennis club really] about 3. Harry came at 4. Barbara, Auntie and I had tea by the river and H joined us before going off to his digs. Dashed home at 7 to get ready for the Châlet. Harry called at 9. Met Eileen and Redmond and spent the evening with them, left them back and went in for tea. Got back home at 2 – Harry didn't go till 4. Gruelling time spent arguing in small circles. Admits to loving me but can't bear seeing me any longer.

Sunday 28

Went for a long drive with Auntie and Mother. Castlewellan etc., lovely day though windy. Harry rang up in the evening and sounded completely normal thank heavens.

Monday 29

Up very late. Went up to the Boat Club with Auntie, Barbara and Heather. Up to the Rink rather late, 7.45 – horribly crowded. H apologised for Saturday night and says it was silly.

April

Thursday 1

Met Eileen at lunch time – late as usual. Handed over my 16 coupons [for the bridesmaid's dress material] and looked half-heartedly at patterns.

Saturday 3

Very busy in the morning: Lionel took me home in the car [ancient cream and red Singer sports]. Up to the Boat Club but only got two sets as it was bitter cold and rainy. Harry came up for a while but didn't play. We had tea together.

Sunday 4

Harry rang me up for a long chat having formulated a new 'hands off' theory.

Monday 5

Very busy with lots of films still coming in for developing. Up to the figure club. Heather there but Harry didn't appear till 9.30 with one of the jeeps. H suddenly sprang it on me that we were going to the Belgravia – arrived and found Comm. B very tight. A large party arrived just back from Dublin and we stayed till after 12. Usual complications ensued afterwards – don't know what to do. Home about 2.30. Bea is engaged.

Tuesday 6

Felt lousy in the morning, also a bit tearful. Bea came in and we looked for patterns. No luck. Pat [Lionel's wife] produced a girl last night.

Thursday 8

Awful crisis at home owing to George being sick and unable to attend the commissioning party – wild proposals left and right. [The unfortunate George had been pressed to accompany my mother.]

Friday 9

Mother fell back on Mr Glenn eventually who is delighted. Awful job getting ready in time. Picked up Auntie's subby at the BCDR station. [Cannot recall the details, but I think some hapless sub-lieutenant had been pressed into service.] Arrived at the ship in good time – everything beautifully arranged – family enjoyed themselves. I kept well out of the way. Harry dragged me around being sociable. Mother etc. left just after 12. We stayed on the ship till 1 then went out to Terence Robinson's in the jeep with Comm. and Mrs B and had a colossal fry. Dumped the other two then Harry took me home and wouldn't go till after 5 and wanted to stay the night. [I am certain that my mother remained awake in her nearby room till she heard sounds of departure.]

Saturday 10

Felt bloody in the morning but very busy at work. Up to the Boat Club about 4 and Harry didn't come till after 5, then he took me down town for a meal.

Sunday 11

Up late - re-did my plait. Harry rang up from the ship and came out for the evening. Said his farewells to Mother.

Tuesday 13

Pretty busy all day. Harry rang up at 6.30 to see if I could do the Ship's Dance after all as he had to go. Called at 8.15 then we went down to the ship and had several drinks. Proceeded to the *Orpheus* about 10. It was terribly rough but rather interesting. Harry took me home in the jeep but did not come in by mutual consent.

Wednesday 14

Took all my clothes into work in a case. Had an awful job getting washed and changed at 5. Mother took me up to the Rink and we saw the Griffiths practising [guest gold medal skaters] - marvellous. Mother dumped me at the Robinsons': Harry was there and we went down to the Grand Central for the dinner dance. Pretty good evening despite the gloom. Came back in a taxi. Harry stayed till 1.30 or so and then I rang for another taxi to take him back. Cried most of the night but terribly glad really for his sake.

Thursday 15

Pretty busy all day which was a good thing as I hadn't much time to be really miserable. Mother insisted on going down to the docks to photograph the *Magnificent* leaving at 1.30. Came home for tea. Mother left me at the Grand Central at 9 where I met Eileen, Redmond and the best man. I think it really was a good party but I just couldn't enjoy it much. All got very merry except me, even though I drank quite a lot. Home at 2.30.

Saturday 17

Busy all morning at work. Mother gave me a compact and a nice travelling sponge-bag for my birthday. Curse arrived thank God.

Monday 19

Ordered two photos from the *News Letter* for Harry and me of the ship. Went up to the Rink – still miserable. Supper with Margaret in her kitchen.

Tuesday 20

No letter from H yet. Felt dreadful all day and terribly inclined to cry. Couldn't face going up to the Rink though I knew I should have – so went to the pictures instead *Mrs Fitzherbert* – bloody awful with Joyce Howard. Got home about 9.30 still not feeling any more cheerful.

Wednesday 21

Pretty busy all day. Got a letter from H – nothing in it as he said and rather dull but lovely. Did the ironing – washed some stockings and wrote a long letter to Harry.

Sunday 25

Woke up feeling lousy. Sat in the garden all afternoon as it was glorious. Made some fudge.

Wednesday 28

Lousy day and very cold again. Met Eileen at the dressmaker's – she liked the dress very much. [This continued to be a sore point with my mother who felt (a) that the material was inappropriate for the pattern chosen; (b) that she could have made it better at no expense; (c) resentment at having had to fork out for the chiffon; and (d) that it was distinctly ill-bred to expect the bridesmaids to pay for their dresses.] Think we can compromise on the headdress question. Eileen getting het up over the sex question. [With justification – the honeymoon was something of a disaster, a doctor's help having to be enlisted.] No letter from Harry yet. Washed hair, stockings and did the ironing.

May

Wednesday 5

Another lousy day. Wedding rehearsal went OK though the church is ill-adapted for weddings. Redmond's mother [the overpowering Bostonian] took Bea and me back to town in the car along with the page and his mother. Finished my letter to Harry at lunch time and got Mother to post it. Still chaos at home altering my frock. Had my hair set at Mrs Lee's [in Cherryvalley village].

Thursday 6

The flowers arrived about 12. Had to tear my headdress to pieces, but it was OK in the end. Down to West's at 1. Eileen looked lovely and everything went without a hitch including the reception. Mother took the bouquets to the UVF hospital. Bea, Virginia, Angus and I hot-footed it up to the GNR and saw them off much to their annoyance. Then I was dumped out home and called for after half an hour by taxi and went to the Midland Hotel where we had a good dinner, after which we went to the Group Theatre and saw *Second Thoughts* – very good. Finished the evening at Redmond's parents' and the best man left me home.

Friday 7

Went along to the WRNS recruiting centre and was greeted with open arms: said they would inform me when the recruiting officer comes over on her next visit. Very sorry I told Mother as it seemed to upset her.

Saturday 8

Up to the Boat Club in the afternoon and went up the river with Cecil and Hugo. [Cecil was at the time consulting Hugo about his concern that girls did not seem to turn him on in the way they did his peer group. He was gentle, and we went to and enjoyed many ballet performances together.]

Tuesday 11

Left my racket in to get the string fixed. Lionel unable to take me over to the Grand Central so went over later with Miss H to carry the tripod. Mucked around till 12.30 or so – awful ordeal – had trouble with the bloody half-plate camera [a model in mahogany and brass dating from *c.* 1910] not focusing at infinity and only found out later what was wrong. [Lionel should never have given me this job to do, which was to record a McLaughlin & Harvey business luncheon. I wince even today at my inadequacy and at the end result, which recorded a sea of sporadically-lit faces that became increasingly distorted towards the edges of the plate.] Up to the club for tea with Eleanor and Norma – still playing badly. More tea later with Heather, Barbara, Morris and Hugo.

Wednesday 12

Lunch in Sherie's and got my Jaegar jacket (no coupon reduction) also a nice white jumper (very expensive). So busy I nearly worked my feet off. Up to the club for tea. Vera was there and I beat her in singles 6-4 – very gratifying after her walloping me in last year's championships.

Thursday 13

Still very busy at work. Gruelling sort of battle with Mother apropos joining the WRNS. [Mother's main concern was that I should become easy prey to unprincipled naval officers.]

Friday 14

Glorious day – sunny and warm. Got a very long letter from Harry – they will be back on Tuesday with any luck.

Tuesday 18

Still lovely weather. Mother took me out to see the tropical fish shop at lunch time. Harry rang up in the afternoon sooner than I had expected, then came round to see me looking very brown and well. Got off about 4.30 and went up to the club for tea with him then played till 9. Down town for supper at the Ritz. Walked to Cromac Square and then parted – he intended walking to Sydenham.

Wednesday 19

Still lovely and sunny. Harry rang about 4.30 from Malone – playing golf with Comm. B. Went up to the club for three sets then down and met H at 8 for dinner at the Grosvenor Rooms. Then we came out home and went for a walk up the Gilnahirk hill. [I well recall the frustration of not being able to find any secluded spot for the bedding down we so much wanted.] Met Fred from the shop on the way back. [So the hunted feeling was well justified.]

Sunday 23

Up pretty late - vile hangover. H rang up at 6 to say he'd be latish. Got here 7.30 - won't be able to see me tomorrow and we had to say goodbye at the bus stop - gruelling.

Monday 24

Busy all day thank God. Lunch with Norma and Vera. Went home in the evening and H rang up at 9.30 for a final chat. Felt utterly miserable and shall not hear for nearly a month probably. [I think this was the end, although H was a conscientious correspondent for a long time. He returned seven years later when I was five years into an unsuitable marriage, and the meeting was not an unqualified success.]

Friday 28

Went to see *The Unfaithful* with Ann Sheridan, Zachary Scott and Lew Ayers - quite good and rather immoral.

June

Tuesday 1

Went to the US Consulate and they gave me the name of the Swiss Consulate in London and Dublin and the Canadian Trade Commissioner here. Spent most of the afternoon at the Museum checking titles and painters of the Old Masters exhib. with Mr Hewitt [John Hewitt - Ulster poet]. Took myself to see *Broken Journey* with Phyllis Calvert, Francis Sullivan and Guy Rolfe. [GR had been a leading member of the only resident dramatic company to play regularly in the Belfast Opera House just after the war. They were called the Savoy Players and I was besotted by GR's emaciated looks – he was reputed to have only one lung.]

Sunday 6

Up very late and did damn all all day. Read *Sense and Sensibility* and ate at intervals. Awful fit of depression when I haven't much to do.

Monday 7

Not a bad day – few showers. Quite a few good matches on. Umpired Heather v. Miss Egan 6-2, 6-3 and made the usual balls of it. [At one time I was unwisely selected to umpire quite an important match between a visiting Czech female and a local girl. I was lucky to survive physical attack from the Czech.]

Tuesday 8

Up to the club and watched for a while. Cecil and I were sent to Falls Road with our opponents N. A. Palmer and Mrs Stone. After we got there they refused us a court. [Start of sectarianism? The Boat Club will have been regarded as a stronghold of middle-class Orange Protestantism.]

Friday 18

Lousy morning – poured for a while. Went to Butcher E [dentist] and had three more fillings. Another very painful wisdom tooth which he said he would have taken out if he had known the hole was so big. Very busy at work. Lunch with Mother and Auntie. Eileen came and talked for a bit. Went up to the Museum to see Princess E's wedding dress – exquisite. [That was not my reaction when I saw it many years later!] Into town to meet the others and see *How To*

Play Tennis at St Mary's Hall, but it was cancelled owing to the wrong film being sent. Took myself to see *Ships with Wings* with Leslie Banks, Ann Todd, Michael Wilding and John Clements. Very good indeed but a bit too much to the point.

Saturday 26

Lunch with Mother and Auntie in the Rainbow. Then A and I went up to the club. Got three sets, then it rained till about 5 during which time we had tea with Barbara, Cecil, David McM and Douglas Hope. Several good sets afterwards and didn't get home till 10.30 dead tired.

Wednesday 30

Barbara called for me at 5.30 and we met Cecil and George for dinner at the Grosvenor Rooms. Then on to the Opera House. The company isn't really much better than a Ballet School – all very mediocre. Out to George's house for tea afterwards and he and Cecil left us home about 12. In very late on account of protracted religious discussion.

July

Friday 2

Dentist: had my last visit to Butcher E till November, he did one small hole and polished all my fillings. Had an unexpected letter from Harry written from his home, quite a long one and lots better than the last. Went to see *The First of the Few* at the Hippodrome and enjoyed it very much.

Monday 12

Dreadful morning, unrelieved gloom and pouring. Up to

the club and had lots of good sets with George, Cecil and Morris. We all got an awful shock in the evening when George had an epileptic fit in the Clubhouse as we had no idea he was subject to them.

Wednesday 14

Back to the grindstone but not too busy. Lionel got back about 12. Up to the club and had another lesson with the coach. Played a set with me and made me feel utterly incompetent.

Sunday 18

Had a very fine filet steak for lunch as a treat. Went down to see San after tea. They have sold the farm [at Donaghadee] making £475 and are going to Donegal in a horse drawn motor caravan which we saw and is very nice indeed. [San's husband had run into severe financial difficulties with his garage in York Street, due to having too trustful a nature and having allowed too much credit. He was also running an illicit relationship with a married woman who claimed that her latest issue was his. This claim, pathetically, flattered his ego. Poor San had suffered a painful late miscarriage in the early 1930s. The situation naturally put a great strain on the relationship, but San's capacity for forgiveness triumphed and they spent the rest of their days in apparent quiet enjoyment of each other's company. After Mr San's death from prostate cancer, the 'issue' visited San and made known his existence. She even accepted this and said he was not at all a bad boy and, 'With that ugly mug, I can quite believe it's his – just like him!']

Saturday 24

Got a long letter from Harry who is back from leave and

hasn't got his promotion unfortunately. [He ultimately became a captain.] Lunch in the Rainbow with Mother and Auntie then up to the club. It wasn't very nice – fine drizzly mist over all. Cecil put in an appearance. Stopped play early. Auntie went to the ballet. I went to the club dance with George, Rowan and Noldred.

Thursday 29

Cecil took me up to the club in the MG. George threw a party later – smoked salmon.

Friday 30

Still glorious and about 80F. Up to the club – Hugo had his girl-friend up and seemed rather repressed. He took her home then came back and took Auntie and me down for coffee at Sherie's. [Hugo was liable to get enmeshed romantically and not know how best, if at all, to extract himself. Cannot remember if this was the one who was too sexually demanding and had hairy nipples or the one he subsequently married.]

August

Tuesday 3

Cecil called and took me up to the club for tea. Hardly saw him after that as Barbara and Auntie appropriated him. [They were late to get the message that C's orientation was not female.] Got another letter from Harry from St Anne's Bay in Cape Breton in a particularly mistrustful frame of mind.

Thursday 5

Auntie got a temporary job as secretary receptionist to Dr

Douglas Boyd. [DB was one of only two radiologists in Belfast at the time. The 'temporary' job lasted something like forty years. Auntie was never paid more than a pittance and took over jobs for which she had no training. This was ethically questionable but she enjoyed the feeling of importance, and her loyalty to DB was resolute.]

Monday 9

Had to photograph a milk van in Howard St in the morning and contend with lots of jeering urchins – quite fun. Up to the club. Eileen off to Dublin for a while. Auntie, Barbara and I came home with Hugo and had chips in the Howard Café first.

Wednesday 11

Up to the Museum to photograph a painting of Wolf [sic] Tone – lovely morning. Called for Mrs B at the Belgravia and we saw *October Man* at the Regal, it was extremely good and John Mills looked precisely like Harry in many scenes. Had a good meal afterwards in the café.

Monday 16

Miss H on holiday and very busy in the shop. Letter from Harry replying to my penultimate one, a bit disgruntled at me leaving a week in between on account of nothing happening. Norma back from Bray. Card from Cecil at Portstewart (very vulgar).

Tuesday 17

Mother set off for the Isle of Man about 5 and should be back on Friday. [She got a contract with the Raphael Tuck postcard firm to take pictures of the IOM. She enjoyed the trip but did not make much out of it.] Auntie and I wrote to two inferior hotels in Rosapenna and Downings. [We intended to make a short trip to that particularly lovely part of Donegal and meet up with George, who stayed annually in the large and expensive hotel at Rosapenna. Our budget was strictly limited.]

Thursday 26

Up at 6.30 and Mother took us to the 8.35 train. Got to Strabane about 12, then an awful little train to Letterkenny [where I remember counting twenty-seven pubs] then a bus to Rosapenna. It rained off and on on the journey but turned out lovely when we arrived. Were met off the bus by a most peculiar individual who took us up to the Villas (frightful place). We soon decided we couldn't stick it and were lucky enough to find another very nice clean place nearby. Walked seemingly miles with our luggage. Went to see George who asked us to dinner tomorrow.

Friday 27

Glorious morning – went for a bathe and lay on the beach. Got a pair of black nylons for 12/11 – lovely. Got the bus into Carrigart and got our ration cards, wrote some PCs and hired two awful men's bikes for 10/- for four days. Mucked about with golf clubs till tea time and then started to get dressed. George called for us and took us to the hotel for a marvellous dinner, but rather too much. Danced till 12.

Saturday 28

Into Carrigart on our bikes to get ration cards. Lovely morning so we went the whole way around the Atlantic Drive at great peril. Bought a pair of nylons for Mother and another pair of black ones. Went to play golf in the afternoon and rescued a bird caught in barbed-wire. Only played four holes and then it rained.

Sunday 29

Very stormy morning. Scrambled around the cliffs and over the headlands to the big hotel – practically blown off at times. George took us for a lovely run [in his silver Jaguar] to Marble Hill and through the monastery grounds at Ards. Auntie caught a large crab but I wouldn't let her bring it home.

September

Thursday 2

Back to work again – chaos in the shop. Went in with Lionel in the bus and he put forward his scheme about putting me in charge of calendars etc. which doesn't really appeal or else doing children. Nominal wage of £3 plus one third of the profits. Not good enough – would rather have a steady, fixed wage. Very awkward. [It *was* awkward, as his family were on social terms with my mother, who had done the 'apprenticeship' deal in the first place.]

Monday 6

Worked till 6.30 then went and met Cecil at the Opera House. We didn't have to queue long and got quite good seats. Mona Inglesby as Odette/Odile in *Swan Lake* – seems improved on last year though very scraggy. Enjoyed it very much and had a meal in the Rainbow afterwards.

Wednesday 8

Still very busy but managed to get out in time to go up to the club. Played with Cecil, Auntie and a new boy called Charles. Only two sets as it now gets dark at 8. Sprained my groin again and my right leg ceased to function completely.

Friday 10

Very busy all day till 6. Had something in Sherie's then went down to the Opera House. Mile long queue at 6.40. Hugo was there at quarter to, but Heather was late and we kept a seat for her. *Sleeping Beauty* with Claudia Algeranova as Aurora. She is really excellent, the dresses were lovely and the corps very good too.

Tuesday 14

Letter from Harry from somewhere near Hudson Bay, rather geographical and not much in it besides. Tea in Sherie's and then down to the Opera House to queue for the Gods. Auntie joined me later and we got very good seats for *Coppelia* with Helene Armfelt as Swanhilda. She wasn't anything like as good as Mona or Claudia.

Thursday 23

Lionel departed for Glenveagh to photograph an American millionaire's castle [this was the Tabasco heir, Henry P. MacIlhenny] and won't be back till Sunday. Lousy day with foggy drizzle over all. Got Cecil a bottle of olives.

Friday 24

Long letter from Harry with two quite good pictures of himself. Rather an ambiguous statement about the 'October arrangement being definitely off'. I don't know if it refers to his family going over to the ship or the ship returning here. Very worrying.

Wednesday 29

Auntie and I went to see *The Bishop's Wife* with David Niven, Loretta Young and Cary Grant. Very amusing though rather bad taste. Also saw the trailer for *The Red Shoes* – looks lovely. Bought 7 yards of rust red moiré for a short evening dress.

October

Sunday 3

Up late as usual. Mr Hughes and Mr Nesbitt came in the afternoon about the bureau and as we couldn't screw any more out of them we had to let it go at £15 which will just about square up my debts. [I have no memory at all of this transaction and fear the bureau referred to may have been one of the two Boulle pieces bequeathed to me by Grandma S. On sale today one would be talking in thousands of pounds.]

Monday 4

Mother's 26th wedding anniversary. [For some extraordinary reason this date was always marked, although it must have brought nothing but painful memories.] Herbie came in to see me in the morning – back from Borneo. He didn't look very well as he had been in the tropical diseases hospital in London for a while with dysentery. [Herbie was a newly graduated engineer whose first job assignment was bridge-building in Borneo. I lost touch with him.]

Tuesday 5

First really frosty night this autumn. Shop front is being repainted and all customers managed to get coated despite large warning notices. Got a *Vogue* pattern for my evening dress. Went to see *Mine Own Executioner* by Nigel Balchin with Burgess Meredith, Kieron Moore and Dulcie Grey which I enjoyed very much. Very long programme and the rest was tripe.

Monday 11

Bought a hat of indifferent quality for 23/– odd. Had tea in Sherie's with Heather and then went up to the rink. Hugo arrived about 8 and took us for coffee. He brought Auntie and me a lovely box of chocolates from Dublin. He seems to be getting cracking on Heather now and is to take her out on Saturday. Had a letter from Harry informing me that they won't be over in Oct. and if they come later he can't as he's been reassigned. [No recorded reaction or tears it seems.]

Tuesday 19

Went down to see Eileen in the evening. Her mother nearly drove me skatty in a short while. Eileen says she's expecting a child in May. All is apparently not quite well and she's been very sick. Succeeded in selling my pearls for £35. [These were real, not cultured, pearls, but very badly matched. Nonetheless I now regret parting with them as my grandfather had bought them for Grandma S.]

Thursday 28

Had a letter from Harry. Seems definite now that he's leaving the ship soon and his new job is in Ottowa. Didn't get away from work till 6.30 owing to dalliance with a rather intriguing man name of Vernon, sorting negatives etc. He took me out for coffee afterwards and I didn't get up to the rink till 7.45.

NOVEMBER

Wednesday 3

Had to take a photo. of a grave at Knockbreda – wasted most of the afternoon. Vernon came in for prints and asked me to go to a lecture by Richard Hayward on 'Recorded Music'. Met him at 7 and he took me for a drink at the

Union Hotel then went up to the Museum. Quite interesting though very short. Took me down town for coffee.

Saturday 6

Had lunch in town and did a bit of shopping then came home. It was such a nice afternoon Mother and I went for a run down to Bangor. Bought a double row of pearls there for 25/- and had a puncture on the way back.

Wednesday 10

Went to see *Mine Own Executioner* again with Vernon who bought me some chocolates and fags. Had coffee afterwards. Talks too much and suffers from youth though quite humorous.

Saturday 13

Lousy day. Had lunch with Mother in the Rainbow. Vernon came in in the morning and arranged to meet me. Auntie and I did some shopping. Got a pair of flat court shoes in a poky shop at Mountpottinger. Met Vernon at 6 and as there wasn't anything on I dragged him up to the Museum to see an exhibition of Irish painting. Spent ages there and then came down for a meal in the Union Hotel. Insisted on leaving me home and I had to ask him in.

Sunday 14

Hugo and Barbara round in the afternoon. Mother cut out my evening dress as V has asked me to the Arts Ball. Princess Elizabeth had a son at 9.14 this evening.

Wednesday 17

Turned out lousy wet day. Met V at the Ritz and saw *Anna Karenina* with Vivien Leigh, Ralph Richardson and Kieron Moore. Not bad but very gloomy.

Thursday 18

Went skating in the evening. The awful youth from the Boat Club put in an appearance and I weakly promised to go to the dance with him – then asked me to go to the flicks on Saturday but of course I couldn't.

Monday 22

Met Mother in town and she came up to the rink for the first time since her accident. She felt very nervous at first but did quite well after that. Left quite early but not before meeting the awful Billy Elliott.

Tuesday 23

Vernon in in the morning for some prints and wasted a lot of my time. He rang up at 11 at night to say he'd found that the dance tomorrow isn't so good and there's a much better one at the Castle on the 6th. Miss H is off ill and Lionel not feeling too good.

Wednesday 24

Met Vernon in the shop at 5.30. Had tea in Sherie's and then went to see *The Blind Goddess* at the Classic with Eric Portman, Hugh Williams and Anne Crawford – very good indeed about a libel case – written by Sir Patrick Hastings. Brought him out home for supper.

Saturday 27

Very busy morning. Lionel out most of the time. Vernon came in and suggested a nice walk. V didn't arrive till nearly 4 after suggesting 2.30! Went for a *nice* walk and got back about 5.30. He stayed to tea despite the fact that he had to go and do some important sketches. Mother and Auntie went to see *The Great Mr Handel* and I spent most of the evening on the floor.

Sunday 28

Hugo and Barbara came round separately in the afternoon. She went at 6 but Hugo stayed on till 11. Heard some of his views on her – he sees pretty well through the mask. Also something rather startling Cecil had said re his possible homosexuality.

December

Sunday 5

Hugo and Barbara round in the afternoon protesting they weren't coming in as they were so wet. However they did and Barbara stayed till 8 or so. Hugo went around 5. Mother getting a bit tired of it I think but nothing I can do.

Monday 6

Vernon in and out all day. Frightful flap about the dance owing to his being broke. Ended by his screwing some money out of a publisher and me lending him £2. He came out about 9 and Mother took us in to the Carlton. Not such a posh dance after all: some weird and not particularly arty types there. Spent most of the time sitting in the bar drinking rum. Frock looks lovely. Have an awful feeling I've lost one of Mother's diamante dress clips but can't think how.

Friday 10

Went to the frightful dance with Billy Elliott. Never encountered a more dull collection of people in all my life. The dinner was lovely but didn't make up for the tedium. Was given an orangeade at 11.30 and a glass of sherry at 12.30. Never more glad to get home.

Tuesday 14

Up to the rink for rehearsal at 6.15. Usual carry on with Sheila S being incredibly dense. However we got as far as mapping out two dances.

Wednesday 15

Went up to Vernon's house for tea – most peculiar family – Mum very queer, Dad quite normal and sister rather unremarkable looking. [Dad was a shipyard worker who liked to read Galsworthy. The house lacked a bathroom and I felt distinctly uneasy – so, probably, did they.] Spent most of the evening on the floor of V's studio. Greatly taken aback by a declaration of feelings about which I was completely unaware. Left me right home and had to walk out from the City Hall.

Friday 17

Very busy all day. Vernon in twice. Went home with Mother and she and Auntie went to *Twelfth Night*. Hugo came over half an hour early and I wasn't even dressed. V came at 9.45 and I gave them coffee. The taxi was late owing to the man falling asleep at the end of the road. The dance was very good though bung full. Hugo says he made a bit of progress with Barbara. Spent over an hour on the top floor. [This must have been the Art School dance in the Belfast College of Technology, where the only place to snog was amid the plaster casts on the top floor of the building.]

Tuesday 21

Met San in town – they are now without a house and practically broke. The caravan trip was unsuccessful and they got no further than County Tyrone.

Wednesday 22

Vernon called for me at 5.30 and we had supper in the Rainbow Room, then went out to his house and talked etc.

Friday 24

Vernon called for me at 5.30 and we went to see a film called *Esther Waters* from a novel by George Moore with Kathleen Ryan: rather poor on the whole though it had its moments. Supper in the Rainbow Room – Vernon gave me a lovely ballet book. [I was subsequently very cruel to V about his sketches of dancers, saying it was all too evident that he had neither training in anatomical drawing nor knowledge of the rudiments of classical ballet positions. This was true, but I fear I did not deliver the message with either sympathy or sensitivity. When it came to depicting buildings and ancient monuments, however, he was naturally gifted. Unfortunately, at that time, I had no concept of a tactful or generous approach to criticism, but this was possibly a ploy to end the relationship with a brutal blow.]

Saturday 25

Very quiet day mainly spent in eating and sleeping it off.

Sunday 26

Up about 11.30. Very busy preparing for the guests. Hugo and Barbara came about 4. Vernon and George shortly after. Unqualified success and all slightly tight by 11. None of them went till nearly 2. [No mention of either Auntie or Mother and I don't know how I got away with the serving of alcoholic drinks, as none was ever kept in our house.]

Monday 27

Up very late indeed. Had still more turkey for lunch. Went

up to V's for tea – more turkey. Usual procedure otherwise. [This relationship did not go beyond heavy snogging. In retrospect I think V had been brought up to respect women and found it hard to believe that 'the ladies might like it after all'. His view was one very commonly held by young males in NI at that time, which led to the lustier females seeking satisfaction elsewhere.]

Tuesday 28

Up late again. Went skating in the afternoon. Auntie and Barbara came as well as Vernon who could just about skate in an indifferent way. He went home to do some work. Met Hugo in the bus home – asked him to come round later – he unburdened himself a good deal about some wild oat he had sown last night and needed advice. Auntie very huffy because she wasn't told too.

Thursday 30

Pretty busy again. Vernon called at 5.30 and we went to *Oliver Twist* with Robert Newton, John Howard Davies, Alec Guinness, Francis L. Sullivan – it really was good throughout. Haven't seen such an undilutedly good film for ages. Took V home for supper. Unpopular with Auntie as usual.

Friday 31

Very busy doing prints for the Textile Testing place. Went up to Vernon's for tea. Did some map tracing for him among other things. Home at 12.15, unpopular again. It has been a memorable year in many ways.

Postscript

My father died in Worthing in 1940. Grandma Stevenson died peacefully in 1947 at her flat in Derry after a short illness. San died in Belfast City Hospital (a place she hated) in 1978, my mother in 1989 in a geriatric ward at Crawfordsburn Hospital (an environment she had always dreaded). Auntie Rosemary died early in 1991 as a result of her chronic asthma, and Annie early in 1995 of old age.